MW01117998

Communication Skills Training

How to Talk to Anyone at Any Time and Read People Like a Book

Christopher Rothchester

counsel, strategies and techniques that may be offered in this volume.

Table of Contents

Introduction

Have you ever been in a public place, and when you needed to speak with someone nearby, you became nervous and couldn't find the right words? Have you ever been trying to read body language but found yourself confused by mixed signals? And have you ever wondered how some people could walk up to strangers and strike up a conversation like it's the most normal thing in the world?

It can sometimes feel like anyone can walk up to you and start a conversation. It's your job to learn how to talk nicely, don't let anyone step up to you and think that it's okay for them to start chatting away. This book will share tips for communicating well with others, from getting past your shyness to reading body language like an expert.

If you're shy, like many others, it will take a bit more than just reading this book. It will require new habits, so you can walk up to strangers and feel comfortable. If you're a person that doesn't like approaching others, then consider keeping an active journal or writing in a diary. This can help with your social skills and conversation skills at the same time. It's good to learn how to have a conversation and have it become more than just talking, so keep at it.

Now, don't be discouraged if you feel like this book won't work for you. It'll take some practice before being able to observe other people and be able to read their body language correctly. This social skill requires time, but it will also need time to apply the skills you learn.

Many people will understand that they're reading this and think, "I've already done this." or "It sounds easy." The first thing they do is go out in public and try their hand at acting naturally in a conversation with another person. It's not as easy as it sounds. First, you have to be able to communicate well with another person. But also, you have to take the time and listen to what the other person is saying. Each conversation is a learning experience, and you don't want to have that experience be something you leave with a bad taste in your mouth about yourself.

Communication can improve your life significantly and make things better for everyone around you. Take the time to try and improve your communication skills and see how it makes you feel. People around you will be happy that you're a kind, friendly person they can talk to at any time.

If you want to improve your social, communication, and conversation skills, then you should pay attention and use your social skills as much as possible. People who don't talk to others often won't get to practice their social skills much, so it's good for them to learn these things.

Communication isn't just about having a conversation with another person. It means making sure that your words reach their intended target meaning is clear and not at all confusing. It also is about reading body language. Someone can be talking to you without learning this skill, but you might not understand what they're saying. When reading body language, you mustn't make assumptions about that person. It's better for them if you let them tell you what's going on than to jump to conclusions.

Once you're able to make a conversation with someone, and it starts with you talking to them, it's even better. That person will feel more comfortable speaking with you, and you'll have the confidence to talk about things that come up for you. It suits your social skills because you've already made a friendly first impression.

Talking to someone is just like anything else. It takes practice to be good at it. But, if you put in the time and effort to research things, you'll be able to learn everything about it in no time. You may feel that it's too difficult for you to speak up and make your voice heard, but this is something that can be easily overcome by putting your thoughts into writing first. It's so much easier to express yourself in writing, and then you can go back and see what you wrote down. If you can make sense of what you said, it will be easy for you to say the same thing out loud.

It's easier for people to speak with others if they know the conversation will be about them. This is one of the essential things in any conversation. Everyone wants someone else to listen to what they have to say. We often can't get this from others because we don't even give them a chance. We don't have time for them or may not even like spending time with others. If you think about others and want them to listen to you, you must ensure they're getting something out of the conversation, too. Pay attention and find out what it is that they like. If they carry a camera, find out if they want to take pictures. If they have a phone, see if they like talking on it or playing games. You can learn so much about others by just paying attention.

Sometimes, people will do things to get attention from other people. One example is when someone makes a scene because someone doesn't talk with them or pay attention to what's happening around them. Another, perhaps more difficult to forgive, an example is someone who pretends not to find something funny or bothersome. Many people don't realize that some people use their body language to signal interest in others. This is why paying attention to how someone else communicates with you is essential.

You can learn so much when talking with others who are different from you. This can be done by asking them many questions about day-to-day life. It's also essential to ensure you're not being a pest when trying to learn about something from someone else. Just because they are willing to talk with you doesn't mean they want to speak with you all the time.

Remember this when approaching others to ask them questions. You don't need to be friends with everyone, and you don't want to be. It's okay to tell someone you aren't interested in being friends or don't want to talk with them because you feel like it's not a good time for you.

It can be challenging for shy people to speak with others. This isn't something that is overcome overnight but can be overcome if you're willing to invest the time and effort necessary. Once you realize how hard work learning social skills can be, you won't mind putting in the time and effort needed. Take the first step by listening to what people have to say instead of thinking about what you will say next. You'll learn so much by listening to what people say.

The conversation can be anything from small talk to deep and meaningful discussions. How you conduct the conversation and what you talk about is different, depending on your social, communication, and exchange skills. Whatever you choose to talk about, it's up to you to lead the conversation. This is something that takes time and practice. Once you learn how to have a conversation, don't be afraid of having a conversation with others. You have social skills if you've learned how to communicate with people!

An essential thing in a conversation is talking and listening. There are many forms of communication, but all of them are important. It's suitable for people who want to become better communicators; they should also work on their body language. If you don't like how someone is talking to you, you can always reject them and tell them how you feel. You never want to be forced into a conversation that makes you uncomfortable. The same thing goes for others as well. If someone talks to others in a way that makes them uncomfortable, it's okay if they reject the person telling them they don't want to talk with them. Communication is about mutual understanding's feelings and body language, so there shouldn't be any hard feelings afterward. Better communication skills make life easier, and people will like you more.

You don't need to know everything about everything. You can learn a lot by asking many questions and then taking note of the answers. Taking things in slowly is good for your brain and social skills. If you're unsure if you can answer any questions, there's no problem with asking them. Having a conversation with someone will always be successful if you learn to get it started first by listening to what they want to talk about and what they don't want. When talking with others, you must speak directly about whatever topic is discussed between you two. It's also important to remember that there are two sides to a conversation, so you can't forget about listening and talking.

Chapter 1: Communication Obstacles and How to Avoid Them

Communication can be the most frustrating and difficult thing in the world. It's one of those things that, no matter how confident you may be, can make you feel vulnerable. We know this is because everyone has different expectations on how a conversation "should" go- but what if we could change that? How? By using a simple technique that is often overlooked when it comes to communication. The right tone, body language, and how you say things are crucial aspects of speaking with others.

What's more, is that you can do this whether you're shy or outgoing; it doesn't matter. However, if you've ever seen someone with extroverted personality traits (those who are naturally outgoing), this technique may seem second nature to them. Great leaders are those who have mastered this skill.

Most will tell you to "be yourself" or "just relax." It may be just a simple thing to say but think about it. How often do you break out of your comfort zone and try something different? It's hard, right? But what if there was a technique that could help you do this?

The key to success is not trying to be someone else but communicating your genuine thoughts, feelings, and opinions. This can be scary and hard at first, but the more you practice, the easier it'll be.

Let's cover some common mistakes most often made when speaking with others. Most people find public speaking one of the scariest things they have to do. There's nothing worse than standing in front of a group of people, sweating, and your mind drawing a blank on what to say next. It's embarrassing and normal to feel this way if you're not confident in yourself or your abilities.

However, this is where the beauty of communication skills training comes in. You can learn how to speak with anyone anytime and read people like a book. It's not easy by any means, but there are some tips and tricks to get you started. Find an opportunity to practice daily with your partner, a work colleague, or family. Regardless of the situation you find yourself in, these tips will help you avoid common pitfalls.

The tone goes a long way when establishing rapport with others. Knowing how to talk assertively is crucial to adding value to others and getting your point across clearly and concisely. Start by using a soft, relaxed tone. This will allow you to speak in a way that those around you will be able to hear and understand. This can be aided by adopting slow breaths and standing with your feet planted firmly on the ground. It's easier for others to understand you when you're speaking clearly, which makes them more likely to listen and pay attention to what you're saying.

Try to avoid any sharp movements or abrupt hand gestures. Your body language can reflect your voice, so if you're speaking in an angry tone, with your arms crossed, or simply jutting out your jaw, they will draw the same assumptions. Take a deep breath, and think before you act. It's hard to do this in scenarios where someone has accused you of something terrible, but overreacting can worsen things.

Being genuine is essential when getting to know others. Don't be too aggressive or standoffish when meeting new people for the first time. A gentle gesture here or there should suffice, rather than saying something rude on purpose or being overly reserved. You may think being mean or harsh to your roommate, friends, or family will keep you from being hurt, but this is a childish way of thinking. People rarely remember the first impression of someone and whether you like it; things will get better over time.

Doing so shows that you're just as dedicated and determined about speaking to others as they are.
In a conversation, you should try to be the one to let the other person know that you're interested in them. This means learning to talk positively about what's happening in your head and life. The goal is for people around you to feel comfortable around you – make them feel welcome and loved by drawing out their best qualities. Never assume they're straight-out rude to you.

Being too aggressive or trying to dominate others makes them feel uncomfortable around you. When it comes down to it, we all want to be accepted and loved by others. No one wants to be disliked or feared, so being assertive is key to establishing trust when speaking with others.

If someone's not getting what you're saying, they may give up on the conversation altogether. It's your job as a leader and communicator to try and understand where they are coming from by accepting their perspective, even if it doesn't match their own. Ask questions instead of attempting to persuade or force your point of view onto them.

Try having an open mind and thinking about putting yourself in their shoes before speaking. This may be one of the hardest things to do, but it's also an excellent way to let go of controlling your emotions. It may be hard at first, but the more you practice, the better you'll get at expressing yourself in a manner that allows others to understand where you're coming from.

Another way to become more confident in your ability to speak with anyone is by practicing how you say things. How you say something can be just as important as what you're saying. You may be saying everything right but pronouncing them wrong. Saying something the wrong way may cause someone to misunderstand you or even make them feel upset.

The main thing is to keep in mind that no one can judge you for being a confident speaker. If anything, people will admire and take notice of your authenticity and character. Even if it's challenging to be yourself, you must realize you're already great at being yourself. How we communicate with others is just as important as the words that come out of our mouths; you can use these tips the next time you find yourself in a public situation. You don't have to feel nervous or intimidated when talking to people. You'll find yourself enjoying time with new people more and more. Dedicating yourself to personal growth is a great way to learn how to speak with anyone. Over time, you'll notice a significant difference in how much more comfortable you feel when socializing with others. This, in turn, will lead you to become more confident throughout the rest of your day; just remember that practice makes perfect.

If anything, these tips should allow you to be yourself and use your natural communication skills. The more you practice, the better you will become at it. Practice like your life depends on it. Follow these simple tips; then, you can become one of those people who can speak with anyone. You may not be able to give an eloquent speech, but you should be able to speak so others understand you and know what you're saying. Always keep in mind that everyone is a potential ally and a potential enemy. Never let your emotions carry the day; you may do more harm than good. The more comfortable and at ease you feel in yourself – the more likely others will feel comfortable around you. Start by doing an excellent job of explaining yourself. If you do this well, it will benefit you in the long run. Never lie to someone; tell them the facts and be honest about your feelings. If you make mistakes, apologize and try to work on fixing them. Don't let others know what makes you feel bad at any time: if they don't care enough to ask, they don't deserve to know.

Others around you must see that there are people who are confident in who they are and how they view the world. Please do your best not to judge others; remember that everyone has a good side and a wrong side, so it's best to keep an open mind when speaking with anyone. Having social skills means gaining the knowledge and confidence to talk with anyone. Being able to communicate with others will not only help you in your career, but it will also help you earn respect and develop lasting friendships. You must convince them there's more to you than meets the eye – they have to see that they can trust you. Speak slowly and carefully – be sure to articulate your words as well as possible. You'll find yourself enjoying time with new people more often, so put these tips into practice as soon as possible.

Here are more tips to help you improve:

1. Listen closely

Pay attention and wait for your turn to speak. It is sometimes frustrating when people don't listen or when they derail a conversation by steering it off-topic. If someone invites you somewhere, respond politely with a yes or no, depending on if your schedule allows it. Don't give an excuse or reason you can't make it because that person will spend the entire night trying to convince you otherwise.

2. Be clear, concise, and to the point.

This doesn't mean you can't be elaborate or involved in the conversation; avoiding going off tangents is essential. When you're talking about something that matters to you, be sure you know where you're heading.

If your message is essential, make others feel it is equally crucial by speaking clearly and confidently. If not, you will appear as if your message is not worth their time and care. Speak with an open mind which includes openness toward other people's ideas and thoughts. When you speak, make your voice heard.

Your voice is an essential tool for communication. Your tone and pitch are what everyone interprets. If your message is unclear, it will sound very dull and unprofessional. So make sure you speak loud enough for everyone to hear you without breaking out into a sweat or whispering, which will only seem like an insult.

3. Pay attention to your body language as well.

When someone speaks to you, they're not looking at you; they're watching you. You may be able to talk, but can you walk the walk? If you don't believe what you are saying, how can others?

Depending on your body language and self-confidence will determine how well you communicate. Stand confidently with your arms at your side. Your body posture should portray confidence. Say what needs to be said without fidgeting or moving around too much.

4. Let others shine as well.

Some people get so caught up in their voices they forget to let others speak. Listening closely is essential, but make sure you are listening and paying attention to the person talking. But it doesn't end there if you are genuinely interested in what another person has to say; your expressions and body language show.
People will value what you say when they see how much value you give to what they say.

The more you practice this technique, the more accessible communication will be. Start by saying "hello" or "how are you?" Remember these tips and notice the difference in how people respond to your words and actions. As you become better at communicating, you will become more confident in yourself and what you have to say. And remember, people will not forget what you said or did, especially when they know it matters most to you. Never forget people will recognize how you interact with them. It is a matter of fact, but it's your choice how you handle those situations.

5. Communicate your thoughts and feelings.

This simple act is what you have to sell and impress others with. However, it may not be that easy. Some people find it difficult to say what's on their minds without putting on a different show.

If you don't feel comfortable sharing your genuine thoughts and emotions, it will be hard for them to believe in you or follow your advice when a problem arises. They may think you are lying or exaggerating a cheap way out of the challenge, but facts are facts; they should know how to react accordingly. Don't compare yourself to others because you will permanently lose in the end; share how good you are now by showing confidence within yourself using this technique.

6. Use the power of visual cues.

Please think of the pictures in your mind and use them to guide your words. For example, if you think of a picture of a mountain, picture yourself as a mountain surrounded by other mountains or wait for the right moment to mention them before you speak about them so that others will feel included and encouraged.

While putting this technique into practice may not be easy, it is something you can do with ease anytime you want to show confidence in yourself and others around you. Be sure not to overlook what others say because they may have valuable advice or suggestions to help build your confidence. It will also help you connect with them and build strong friendships.

A good conversation starter can be the difference between making an impression or just going through the motions. On the other hand, if you don't know how to start a conversation, you probably won't be able to carry one on. Whether during work or in your free time, make sure you are prepared for those conversations by practicing these essential skills and tips for speaking. It is not always easy to know whether to speak or listen because being a good speaker is hard to learn and takes practice. Speaking confidently and skillfully will allow others to see your abilities and trust you with their feelings.

7. Rehearse in advance.

Practice these techniques the day before a big meeting, and memorize everything you want to say. If you do it in advance, you will have time to rehearse when it's time to speak.

When practicing, it is best to visualize yourself standing confidently and confidently speaking your thoughts. Bitterness can creep in if someone talks negatively about what they think of you, even though that person should not have said anything because they do not know you yet.

8. Organize ideas for your speech.

Avoid looking at the floor; look straight ahead or at the person being addressed. Make sure you need to say what you have to say when it is time to speak. If not, let someone else have the floor and step back. This will ensure that those not speaking listen closely to your words by giving them their full attention.

9. Plan to speak last.

It is best to say what you have to say after everyone has had their turn. If you try to put in your two cents before everyone has spoken, your ideas may be misinterpreted as trying to take over the conversation. Instead, stand back and let others say their minds first; listen closely and keep an open mind as they talk. This will allow you to judge what they are talking about and how they feel by the tone of their voice or facial expression. Once you are sure it is your turn to speak, stand confidently in front of the group and deliver your message with clarity and conviction.

Communication should not be an obstacle to building rapport and strengthening relationships. So, the next time you are faced with a situation that requires you to speak with others, remember these tips and use them to your advantage. It is essential to not only listen to others but also hear what they say, so make sure you focus on them and try not to get distracted by your surroundings. Never forget that communication is a two-way street. If you do not listen carefully and attentively, you will never be able to understand what others are telling you.

Chapter 2: Expressing Anger and Managing Conflicts

We all know how difficult it is to talk to someone who consistently makes you angry. Whether they're arrogant or just rude, they can make anyone feel frustrated and lash out at them in return. But instead of conceding to their bad behavior and isolating yourself, you should learn how to communicate with people better — especially when there's a conflict brewing between the two of you.

Communication is key to resolving any conflict. If you can find a way to resolve the issue with someone without breaking down, blaming each other, or losing your temper in the process, you'll make everyone's life easier. When it comes down to it, you'll need to talk through your problems and try to sort everything out with some compromise.

The truth is that talking to someone who makes you angry or frustrated isn't easy. It's hard to remain calm and collected, and your emotions tend to get the best. The hardest part is being able to disagree with them honestly and respectfully. You can't shout or become hostile towards someone if they're going to listen to what you have to say — especially if what you have to say is something they don't want to hear.

Some people may be more challenging to talk to than others (i.e., those who are consistently negative or rude), but there are ways to talk to anyone, regardless of their personality. It might take some time, but you can communicate with any person if you know how.

The essential part of communication has clear, defined boundaries. Have a firm personal limit before talking to someone who makes you angry. Think back to the last time you argued with someone; did they ever try to push your buttons? Were they trying to get you to lose your temper? Or did they wait until you're on the edge of losing it before saying anything?

This is important because refusing to listen or reacting violently when someone pushes your buttons is dangerous and unnecessary. When you know how the other person is trying to manipulate you, you can then choose whether or not you want to listen or fight back.

And even if the other person isn't trying to manipulate you, it's still a good idea to have firm boundaries. If someone keeps pushing your buttons, they're likely trying to make you angry — but if what they're saying isn't affecting how you feel about them, why should you respond with anger?

Once your boundaries are clear and defined, it's much easier for you to talk clearly and respectfully to whoever is making your blood pressure rise. You'll also understand what they're trying to say when they're being rude or pathetic.

Always stand up for yourself (don't let people walk all over you). Lots of people love being rude without even realizing it. Whether it's because they think being condescending or snarky makes them look witty or attractive or because they're too wrapped up in their own lives to care about yours, you shouldn't let other people treat you like crap.

Do you know what's essential? Being a good person and doing right by other people. How you interact with them and how they treat you are equally important; if someone makes your life difficult out of meanness or ignorance, then they don't deserve your forgiveness — especially if the problem could have been easily fixed in the first place.

Don't let people walk all over you. If someone's being disrespectful or hurtful towards you, stand up for yourself as soon as possible. You won't just be making yourself feel better about the situation positively (you'll also be taking away their control over how your day goes). Still, you'll set an excellent example for everyone else to follow and teach them the importance of treating everyone equally.

Keep an open mind. It's easy to get angry when listening to someone who won't stop talking about something that doesn't matter to them or someone who only has bad things to say about everything. It's even easier to be rude or condescending toward them.

But being open-minded and friendly with everyone, no matter how positive their attitudes are, is difficult. It can sometimes get boring to talk to people who only have good things to say. You can't maintain an open-minded attitude towards everyone and everything in life, but you can keep it regarding non-negative people. All they want to do is enjoy their lives and be happy without putting up with terrible attitudes from others (i.e., you). So keep an open mind for a change, regardless of how boring or negative the other person is at times. You never know when something exciting or positive might come out of that conversation after all. If it's hard for you to talk to someone who makes you angry/frustrated, don't feel bad about it.

The more you try to control your anger and frustration, the worse you'll feel — and that's just not healthy. If something is making your blood pressure rise, it's worth trying to figure out what the problem is — and if other people are being rude or hurtful towards you, then, of course, it's worth standing up for yourself in a way that doesn't involve fighting back.

But everyone has had times when they've been frustrated or angry with someone but didn't say anything. Maybe they were scared of what would happen if they did say something (i.e., the other person would react violently), or perhaps they were so angry that they couldn't trust themselves to talk correctly.

It happens to everyone; even the best people in the world have trouble expressing themselves sometimes. If you feel like you can't talk to someone because it's too hard, that's perfectly fine — just focus on becoming a better person in the future and avoid unnecessary arguments with anyone.

Don't let anger consume you. Whether you're trying to communicate with someone who won't listen or if your problems are getting out of hand, remember that losing control isn't worth it — especially when it comes to other people.

Here are some tips on how to communicate better if you are feeling hostile:

1. THINK BEFORE YOU SPEAK

Most of the time, you'll want to speak your mind immediately. But if you have a heated argument with someone (whether it's a coworker, parent, or significant other), you need to make sure that what you're about to say is worth saying. If not, then don't say anything at all.

It's always better to stay silent than speak when you're angry — because the more time passes, the more rational and calm you feel. Don't speak up until you have the facts and can honestly express yourself. You don't have to go off on someone to make a point — you can calmly explain your opinion and tell them why you feel the way you think.

To get yourself to stop and listen to someone, try this trick: Count down from 10 in your head before speaking. By the time you hit zero, you'll be able to express yourself without completely confusing or angering the person on the other end.

2. GET SOME FRESH AIR

If talking about whatever it is that's bothering you makes you feel stressed out or anxious, then take a break from each other instead of continuing the conversation. Do something else for a little while — like take a walk outside or play a game on your phone — and then come back to each other when you're more relaxed.

When it comes down to it, communication is all about two people being able to listen and pay close attention to each other without feeling hostility. Sometimes that's hard to do, so if you're feeling too stressed out, then you'll have a better time if you can just hang out alone for the time being.

3. GET IN THE RIGHT MIND SETTINGS

Sometimes we don't want to hear the truth about a situation because it's too difficult to handle, or we know that what we are about to say will hurt someone's feelings. If you're one of those people, you'll want to ensure that you're in the right frame of mind before speaking to someone.

It's not always easy to do this. You may have to meditate a little bit and clear your head before getting centered. You also need to ensure that you're in a comfortable location, like turning your phone off so that you won't be distracted by any other messages or calls. And if the person making you angry is physically present, try to step away from them and take a break for a little while before attempting to talk things through.

4. LISTEN MORE THAN YOU TALK

You know what to do. You're about to speak your mind, but instead of showing the other person you're upset or angry, try to make a point.

Remember: listening is the best way to get your point across. When you tell someone something, and they interrupt or criticize what you said, it will make them feel more annoyed towards you than ever before. If you can soak in all of what the other person has to say, then there's a greater chance that he'll respect you more for being respectful.

5. BE PATIENT

You shouldn't speak up like a short-tempered older man — that's just going to piss the other person off. If you want to express your feelings, then it's best to try to be as patient as possible. Instead of telling them what you think, try to help the other person understand where they went wrong.

For example: if someone says that they don't like how you did something, you can tell them instead: "I understand. I went faster in turn and lost control of the vehicle."

6. TELL THE TRUTH

Yes, even if it's hard for you to speak about the situation. Even if it hurts to say — especially if it's someone you love or care about deeply — you need to take responsibility for your actions. By not being honest with yourself or the other person, there's no way they will be able to trust or respect you.

There is a time and place for everything, but sometimes life sucks, and things go bad. We tend to say the wrong things and make bad decisions. But it's not about being the wrong person — it's about surviving in a world where people aren't always friendly to each other. And that's okay, as long as you know how to handle yourself and how to act when tempers are running high.

7. ALWAYS HAVE AN EXIT STRATEGY

If things start getting super intense, you need to be able to call a time out — whether that means leaving the room or having the friend with you distract the person on the other end so that you can take some time for yourself.

It's always best if you can handle your feelings without the other person having to know they're affecting you negatively. It's not easy, especially if you want to tell someone something, and no matter how hard you try, it doesn't get said at all.

But the only way to happen is if you have an exit strategy. There's no use in staying in a room if things are terrible. And even if all politics is just a game to you, it doesn't mean that you don't have feelings like everyone else does — and they should be heard as well.

8. BE THE FIRST TO APOLOGIZE

Sometimes life is just messy and complicated when it comes to communication. Sometimes people don't like hearing what you have to say because it hurts them knowing you're upset or angry with them. And sometimes, people take what you say the wrong way without you even knowing.

If this is the case, it's always best if you're the first to apologize — especially if you didn't mean anything wrong to happen in the first place. If there was a misunderstanding, then clear that up as soon as possible by saying sorry.

If there was no misunderstanding, you still need to take responsibility for your actions and say that you never meant for the situation to occur. A quick way to transform hostility into cooperation is to take responsibility for your actions. If you didn't tell, the other person would be mad at you, then say it. If you want to apologize for something, then do it. If you didn't think the situation would go wrong, then say it. Sometimes life is messy and chaotic — and sometimes we say things we don't mean or hear something like that said to us.

If you can apologize for your actions in a way that's calm and honest, then it's likely that the other person will forgive you. And if they don't want to talk to you anymore, then at least you can walk away from the situation knowing that you did everything you could to resolve the conflict peacefully.

The power of empathy and forgiveness
When you know how to express yourself and make the other person feel comfortable, it can be easy to find an understanding and give each other more respect.

We all want people to listen when we talk, but many of us don't know how to do that properly. We're afraid of hurting someone's feelings, and we're too scared to say things that might hurt someone's feelings because we don't want them to think badly about us.

But it doesn't have to be like this. If you can learn how to express yourself well, you can be thoughtful about what you say, even if it makes the other person mad. And this will allow both of you more opportunities in the future.

You never know how much something that seems little could mean something big — especially regarding communication and relationships. People often think it's easier to be empathetic than logical. But using empathy to resolve conflicts gives you the power to turn a negative situation into a positive one. When you can learn how to communicate better with those around you, you'll become more confident and have more power over your life.

Even if you don't always get what you want, at least you can learn when to walk away without having to be held hostage by your own emotions.

The people who stay angry with others are the ones who don't know how to say sorry and accept the feelings of others. And if you're able to use empathy as a gift instead of a weapon, then both sides can try and make peace even if they don't feel like it in the end.

The reality is that most conflicts grow big because people cannot handle them well. Even if you don't like the situation, at least you can learn how to communicate with others in a way that avoids many difficulties.

Suppose you can learn how to have rational conversations that lead to friendly conversations. In that case, you'll be able to resolve conflicts with other people quickly. Communicating better means letting go of your emotions — but you don't have to do it alone. Then you can learn to share without upsetting the other person and without allowing anger to build up inside you until it explodes.

Many people don't like conflict, especially if they think it will leave them angry and stressed out for a long time. But one thing is for sure — if you're going to learn how to get along on any level, then it's necessary for both parties involved.

By learning to communicate better and use empathy instead of anger, you can find a way to turn a negative situation into a positive one. Once you can do that, you can find solutions that you and the other person will be able to live with.

It's not easy — but it is possible to have good relationships with people. All it takes is patience, an open heart, and the ability to communicate your feelings without letting them get in the way. The sooner you learn how to do this, the sooner your life will become more accessible and less stressful — because instead of focusing on the negative things around you, you'll learn how to find solutions for what goes wrong.

Chapter 3: Reading Faces and Predicting Behavior

Your face and your body send out thousands of signals every day. These signals indicate what you are thinking, how you feel, what you want from others, and what you plan to do. These signals are enormously influential in establishing connections, influencing behavior, and achieving goals. You send out these signals without even being aware of it. You constantly read and react to other people's faces and body language, making judgments that affect your feelings, thoughts, and actions.

As soon as you wake up in the morning, you look in the mirror and respond to your facial expressions. Besides impacting how you feel, your facial expressions affect how others think of you. If you are tired, angry, or sad, you will make a negative face that makes you feel worse. Conversely, if you smile at yourself before going off to work or school, it will probably put a smile on your face throughout the day.

Research has proved that how you sit, stand, hold your head, move your hands, and walk can suggest your trustworthiness or competence. Your body also sends out facial signals that others pick up on without your awareness. Open body language—arms uncrossed, palms visible—says "I'm honest and approachable.

Most people, even those with high communication skills, aren't aware of how much they're signaling to each other. You may over- or under-react to someone's facial expressions. Your body language could send mixed messages and make you appear nervous or aggressive even when you're not feeling the old way. You may be unaware of how much you infuriate others by being too direct. How do you know what someone else is thinking?

Your face and body are like a window into the mind, each giving off messages that are hard to decipher on their own. The more you understand how to read people and predict their behavior, the more effective your communication will be.

Reading body language
You should be aware of people's body language so you can better understand their thoughts and feelings. Knowing other people's body language will improve your ability to understand them, predict their actions and behavior, and build strong relationships. You can also use this knowledge to make yourself more appealing as a conversational partner.

People are constantly sending out signals from facial expressions to posture to gestures. The person may scowl, hold his head high, clasp his hands tightly together, look down at the ground or up at the ceiling, and twist his body in. Many alerts are being sent out all the time, which can still be hard for you to read and understand.

You don't have to be a social psychologist or expert in human behavior to read other people's body language correctly. Here are some simple guidelines to help you interpret and respond effectively. People often feel anxious or uncomfortable when they have to interact with others. They usually take several deep, cleansing breaths and tense up their bodies. Watch how people cross their arms, legs, and feet. They may tuck their hands under their armpits or cross their legs in front of them. Be aware of what people do with their hands because they send out necessary signals when they put them in certain positions.

Pacing is a sign of nervousness or anticipation. When you see someone pacing around the room, you can assume that they are apprehensive about something upcoming. If you get up to go to the bathroom during a job interview, notice how the interviewer's body language and behavior change as soon as you leave the room.

Don't overlook the importance of posture and facial expression to indicate what someone is thinking. People tend to follow one another's lead unconsciously, so if your boss sits behind his desk and crosses his legs, you will follow suit and do the same thing. You know that now it is time for business, not casual conversation.

The next time you're in a public place like a restaurant or theater, pay attention to how people react when they walk into a group. They will usually find a place to sit halfway between the most dominating and weakest people. If you are in a meeting, try to observe the seating arrangements. People usually sit next to people they like or are comfortable with.

The next time you're at a party, listen carefully to what people say when they introduce themselves to someone new. Very few people will say anything negative about themselves, even though they may talk negatively about others. Observe how casually people shake hands. The stronger the grip, the more dominant and confident they feel while shaking hands with you—which may indicate how tough they really are.

You can use the same technique for another reason: to see how confident people are about a specific topic or subject. If you know what mood a person is in, you will have an easier time guessing what he might be talking about when introductions are made.

Before you go out with friends the next time, watch how much weight one person distributes evenly across his feet and hands as he walks so that his center of gravity is nice and even. He will walk like he has nothing to prove. If you ever get into an argument with someone, and he tries to pick either one of your hands up at the wrist, it tells you he is feeling vulnerable and insecure about something.

When greeting someone, look at his feet and notice how they're pointed. If they are pointed toward you, it is a sign of openness and confidence; if they are pointed away from you, it is a sign of rejection or defensiveness. Watch how straight a person stands up when talking to someone he's attracted to. He will stand much more straightforwardly than usual because he will try to look as attractive as possible.

When people stand with their arms crossed in front of them, this is a sign that they are blocking themselves off from the world. They feel turned off by what's happening around them and are not interested in getting involved in anything that might happen. People who cross their arms in front of them often do it because they feel vulnerable, insecure, or insecure about something.

A person who leans his face toward you to talk may be trying to get closer to you physically or may just be emphasizing what he is saying by extending himself outward. The opposite is true when a person pulls away from you and crosses his arms tightly with his hands in fists. These are signs that this person was not receptive to your ideas then.

Here are five body language tips:

1.) Keep your feet planted on the floor while talking to someone else unless walking is necessary. The more comfortable and confident you appear, the more others will be drawn to you.

2.) Smile and laugh often, even if you don't feel like it. Even if you are not having a good day, make a conscious effort to force yourself to smile more. A smile is one of the best ways to make others feel good about themselves and for you to come across as a warm, caring person.

3.) Make sure that your eyes are focused on the other person and that your head is at an angle (not straight up or down). These two things will help show your interest in what the other person is saying and help move the conversation along more smoothly.

4.) If you find yourself in situations where someone else's body language sends negative signals, do not mirror them. If you push back by crossing your arms, leaning away from someone, or turning down your neck and facial expression, you're only making yourself look like a less confident person. You will make it harder for the other person to be drawn toward you and feel comfortable.

5.) Pay attention to the way that people talk in a light and friendly tone (never using the word "like" or "as if"). Remember that no one will notice any minor changes you make on your own. The most important thing is to listen intently, not just hear what others are saying.

Body language can be divided into three general categories: behavioral, ritual, and emotional. Here is an example of how each category would be read:

Behavioral—A person in this category would approach you with a friendly smile, open stance, hands on hips, leaning slightly forward, and shaking or tapping their foot in rhythm.

Ritual—This person may stroll to get closer to your conversation with exaggerated hand gestures or fingernail polish. He may rub his chin the entire time you talk and turn his head slowly from side to side like a bird looking for worms.

Emotional—The person in this category may move closer to you, lean their face toward yours, or open their hands and place them on your arm when he talks to you. He may be afraid of something or unsure of what he is saying.

The key to reading body language is to tune into all three categories by looking for signs from each type. Of course, we want to ensure that we're picking up on the non-verbal cues, not what someone said. By understanding these concepts, you'll be a better judge of what's happening around you and better understand how to gauge people's moods and responses.

When someone is speaking, study the way their mouth moves. Does it move too fast or too slow? Does it open wide at certain intervals? What are their hands doing during the conversation? Do the person's arms move in a coordinated manner with their speech, or are they swinging wildly back and forth as they talk?

You should also pay attention to whether their facial expressions match the words they're saying. Does their mouth seem to be grinning, frowning, or smiling? What eyebrow patterns are they using? Are they making sudden changes in their expression?

A person expressing much emotion while someone else is speaking to them will often lean forward or turn away from you and make sudden loud noises. If the person's face turns red or whatever color their face turns, this is a clear sign that they want to be left alone.

This sign can be easily seen by scientists and researchers studying stereotypes. They have noticed a correlation between how long a person has been doing something before performing it perfectly and the time it takes for him to get good at it. If a person has been doing something for ten years and is still not very good at it, it is a sign that they have not been applying to it. Here are essential things to remember when reading body language:

1. Be skeptical of everything you read. Your first reaction when hearing a piece of body language advice will be to agree with it completely. If you take yourself out of the picture and attempt to apply that same bit of information to another person, however, you'll be able to tell if it is useful.

2. Don't focus on one person and expect them to give off specific body language cues all day. Instead, be sensitive and feel what's going on around you while also working on keeping your body language in check.

3. Do not engage in stereotypes. This is a big no-no in reading body language because stereotypes are dangerous. If someone is telling you something is true based on their color, gender, sexual orientation, or any other type of bias, then you do not want to believe it.

4. Pay attention to non-verbal cues as well as verbal ones. Saying anything can be said in non-verbal language, and if you're able to pick up on these cues, it will make understanding how someone's body language works that much easier for you.

5. Let people speak when they wish and listen more than talk. When someone is speaking to you, do not interrupt unless you have something significant to add. When someone is speaking, move your body and facial muscles to show that you are listening.

6. Always remember that everyone has a story to tell. You may have an opinion about what's happening with another person, but if they don't want to talk to you or make eye contact with you, then do not persist in prying them for information. It will only get in the way of them telling their story on their own time and probably ruin it.

7. Only observe touching if you feel comfortable with it. When you see someone touch another person, this is a clear sign that they are satisfied with them and feel safe around them. This is not something that everyone wants to do, and it's not something that everyone should do, so don't force yourself into physical contact with anyone who you don't feel is willing to give it to you.

8. Do not judge people until you know their backgrounds and why they act the way they do. Remember, everyone has a story to tell, but only they know how it will end up for them in the future.

9. Let go of any baggage you may have. If you have a history with someone, allow him or her the opportunity to show you his or her new side even though they might not seem to be the same person as they once were or even the same person you once knew.

10. If you see something wrong, do not be afraid to speak up. Have an opinion of what's going on around you or with one person and say something rather than making a judgment on your own. Remember, everyone is flawed.

In this day and age, it is essential to understand people's nonverbal behavior. Reading faces and predicting behavior based on nonverbal cues can be difficult, but it is worth it if you want to improve your interpersonal interactions. Otherwise, you might make many mistakes that could have been avoided. The key to the successful reading of body language is to remember what you see and what others see and that different people will react differently to the same situation. Each person has their version of the truth, and you must learn how to adapt yourself to read their body language effectively.

Nonverbal cues are important because they are one of the main ways that people communicate with each other. By reading their nonverbal cues, you'll be able to understand the situation and how to respond to it. You'll also be able to tell how that person is feeling and what they will say next. While it may seem daunting at first, the skill of reading body language is not as difficult as it looks. Once you improve, you'll find that understanding other people's body language feels much more natural. You will be able to see the hidden cues and understand their responses instantly without any difficulty or misunderstanding. You will feel confident in your ability to read body language and know exactly how to act based on your nonverbal cues.

Chapter 4: Giving and Receiving Feedback

Feedback is a vital component of effective communication. It is central to understanding what is happening in the conversation and ensuring that both parties are represented. When feedback becomes difficult, it comes down to a lack of confidence and practice. Feedback is a critical component of any negotiation or relationship; your ability to give and receive feedback makes the difference in negotiating for better deals, getting a job done, or making a sale. It is the skill that helps you to improve your skills and make you a better salesperson.

Feedback is vital to effectively communicate with others because it allows you to respond appropriately. Feedback is the difference between "I think you are wrong" and "You are wrong." Using the feedback that someone has given you allows you to learn how others perceive situations differently than yourself. Feedback also enables you to remember what someone has said rather than assume they are telling the truth as they see it, which can be detrimental to negotiations.

Feedback is a skill that cannot be perfected overnight, but with practice, it will become an integral part of your communication style.

Step 1: Critique the performance of others.

Learn from your feedback and remember when making your subsequent evaluation. Having critiques done on yourself may be difficult, but when you start critiquing others, avoid putting your personal feelings into it and focus on the facts of their performance when making your evaluations. Evaluate them by their performance, not their personalities.

Step 2: Learn to listen to others effectively.

Learn how to listen to get more information and clear communication necessary to be successful in any interaction. Listening is an essential skill to learn when working with others, as it allows you to understand what the other person is saying. When listening, you should: 1) Listen to interruptions, 2) not make judgments based on your perspective, and 3) Take time to understand what is being said. For example, if someone says, "The meeting was terrible. The room was too cold." You may respond emotionally to the comment and ask, "which room?" or "What was wrong with the meeting?" The person may say that the client wanted a warmer environment, and you did not deliver it. This statement may be a request for feedback from you that you can use to help improve your next interaction.

Step 3: Practice active listening skills.

Active listening is another essential skill that helps you get information about what is happening in the interaction. Active listening allows you to understand whether what someone is saying is true. For example, when someone is talking, you should: 1) Be fully engaged in the conversation, 2) Make eye contact with the speaker, 3) Understand their feelings and opinions by reflecting them to them, and 4) Take notes on what is being said. To effectively communicate your ideas, it is important to listen well.

Step 4: Be fully engaged in the conversation.

Being fully engaged allows the other person to feel that they are being heard and that they are being given your complete attention. It can also make people think that you do not want to be there and will not be a productive interaction. Staring at your phone or checking a watch without the effort to be involved in the discussion can be construed as disinterest and disconnection.

Step 5: Understand their feelings and opinions by reflecting on them.

When you are listening empathetically, it allows the other person to feel that they have been heard. By putting their feelings into words, the person cannot help but have those words reflected on them. You should mirror or empathize with what the speaker is saying by using "I see" or "I understand." This will give the speaker a sense of being understood and erase any chances they may have misunderstood or misinterpreted.

Step 6: Take notes on what is being said.

Taking notes during an interaction to summarize what is being said will help you to remember the discussion and keep you focused on what is being discussed. Taking notes will help you focus more on the conversation and improve your active listening skills. It will also allow you to review what was agreed upon, which may be helpful for follow-up or future communications with the person.

When to use feedback

"When to tell someone that they are wrong? It is important to always recognize that people make mistakes. You should always provide feedback when they do something wrong. The worst thing you can do is not identify when someone makes a mistake or have access to feedback when trying to improve. The right time frame varies depending on the situation, but it should be within your first few interactions with someone."

Receiving feedback is essential in making you a better communicator. Receiving feedback allows you to understand how others see situations differently and help you define better what works and what does not work for them. Receiving feedback can also help you improve your skills and make you a better communicator.

Reflect on feedback when someone gives you feedback and ask them for clarification. This will allow you to understand what they mean. Taking time to reflect on the feedback will help you to improve your communication skills.

Here are some things that you should do to receive feedback:

1.) Have a purpose for the meeting before and during. Know why you will be talking with this person. For example, if you are meeting with a customer service representative and are dissatisfied with their performance, understanding why it is essential that this person is there will improve your interaction.

2.) When making requests of others, make sure that your request is for a specific action to get an accurate response from them. It may be helpful to define the incident or situation to clarify what you want the other person to do and prevent misinterpretation of your request. For example, "I would like to have my order shipped by noon. It is evening, and I have not received a shipment confirmation or tracking number."

3.) Listen to what the other person has to say. Their suggestions and comments may provide you with information you did not know about the situation.

4.) Summarize what you heard from the other person to clarify the message that you heard from them. After listening, reflect on their feedback by summarizing what you hear them saying so that they can confirm or deny your summary. This will allow for a clear understanding of their thoughts and opinions.

5.) Repeat any critical information so they can verify whether or not you understood what they were trying to say. Repeating back to them will prevent you from leaving out any important messages.

6.) Verify that they agree that the issue has been resolved by asking them, "Did I do a good job with this feedback?" or "Is this something that we can agree on as being resolved?" This will allow the other person to verify whether or not you truly understood and "fixed" their problem.

7.) Thank the other person for their time and feedback to show your gratitude for their interaction. Showing gratitude will help you maintain a positive relationship with this person, and they may be more likely to work with you again.

How and where to provide feedback

"Knowing how to give feedback is important when working with other people. Knowing how you should give feedback will help you ensure that you are getting your point across and that the other person knows that you are trying to improve the business or whatever situation you may be in. Feedback might not always be positive, but it is essential to growing as a professional and ensuring that your work is fulfilling its purpose."

We give and receive feedback in many places in our everyday lives. Giving feedback can happen anywhere from a classroom setting to online social media interactions. We often communicate through written and verbal means in our day-to-day lives. For example, oral and written communication can give feedback at work.

Setting up an informal or formal meeting will lead to how you deliver your feedback. A formal meeting may require more questions than employees' relaxed, friendly atmosphere. If you are taking notes for a forum in which the input will be given, make sure you consider the other person's situation and the tone of the discussion.

When you receive feedback, you may be excited about your progress and feel that you have done a great job, but it is essential to remember that receiving feedback is not always the goal. You can still be thankful for the input and not let it become a distraction from what is happening in your life.

Here are some tips on how to provide feedback:

1.) Look for the best way to provide feedback so it will be received correctly by the other person. Here are some ways that you can give feedback:
a.) Directly put your thoughts into the world so they will be heard and understood by the other person.
b.). Illustrate your thoughts and concerns through examples from a situation you are working on.

c.) Sharing written notes of things you have observed or done will help express your understanding of the situation. You can read these tweets or emails to the other person and let them know through these notes of your observations about their work or feedback about work that you feel is important.

2.) Read each person's reaction - to see whether or not they understood what was said. If not, re-word it in a way that is clear and easy to understand for the other person.

3.) Question if the other person feels the same way. This is essential to ensuring that you are on the same page and truly understand what they are trying to say and want.

4.) Thank them for their time and their opinion. This will show your gratitude for what they have said and done.

5.) Make sure that you think about what was said to you and reflect on it. Use this as a way to improve yourself as a communicator in the future by seeing your own mistakes and noticing how other people communicate with you.

6.) Remember that feedback is not just something that happens at work, but you give and receive feedback in your everyday life. Critique your communication with others to become a better listener and communicator.

7.) How do you give feedback? What tips would you like to share with other people?"

Feedback is often seen as a necessary evil in most situations, although it can be a valuable tool. There are many ways that feedback can be effective, both positive and negative. Below we will discuss how to use feedback effectively in various situations.

Positive Feedback

Positive feedback is a great way to compliment someone for doing their job well and providing good customer service. Positive feedback also encourages the other person to do their best work because of your positive attitude toward them. Having this type of relationship with your coworkers can help you become a stronger team player and leader within an organization. Use this situation to share a positive note with your coworkers by simultaneously using both positive and negative feedback. It is important to note that both types of feedback should be delivered with a friendly attitude and an understanding of the situation.

When giving positive feedback, it is a good idea to provide examples of what you have seen that person do well for others in your organization and customers. This will show your employees and team members that you are paying attention to their work and still showing them that you appreciate their efforts daily.

Giving negative feedback will help to show that you are not afraid to speak up and honestly express your concerns about the product, the process, or the employee. Negative feedback should be delivered in a friendly manner, as well as a professional manner. Negative feedback is often used to ensure that employees perform their jobs correctly and do what they are told to do. Therefore, negative feedback should always be given with an understanding of how some products or services can end up being a problem for customers in the long run.

Accordingly, negative feedback can be crucial for an organization to understand why certain products are not working out for their customers. Also, it becomes easier to fix the problem and improve on them so that they will work correctly in the future. Negative feedback can be given in many forms: verbal feedback, written notes, and feedback through social media. This can help to show that you are taking the time to give your employees feedback during a meeting, but also through other methods of communication.

Please note that negative feedback can sometimes be difficult for employees. Try not to give negative feedback through email or phone because these mediums can make it seem like you are just not interested in them or their work. Additionally, most employees will become defensive when criticized because of how highly they usually view themselves compared to their coworkers. It can be a good idea to avoid giving negative feedback in person.

One of the best ways to understand how you should give negative feedback is to ask your friends or coworkers what they have seen from you or others in your company. Ask them to share with you both positive and negative aspects of their jobs so that you can see what types of things you do that are acceptable and not acceptable for the organization. This can help you to be more effective when giving critical feedback because it will not appear like you are only speaking negatively about someone's performance when in reality, there are many different ways that people can improve their work product.

When discussing negative feedback with your employees, try not to use too much emotion in your verbal communication. This can help your employees not feel so defensive about what you are saying and will help you be a better listener. Open up the conversation between you and your employee about the negative feedback by asking them how they feel about their work, products, or services they deliver to customers. This way, you can open up a dialogue with them before giving your feedback so that they do not feel like they have been blindsided by it. This will also allow them to understand you better as a leader and help the employee understand where their performance is going wrong in certain situations.

Chapter 5: Building Rapport, Networking, and Creating a Unique Personality

Rapport is a vital communication skill. It requires giving the other person your full attention and being interested. Additionally, it's about matching their body language, attitude, and tone of voice. Rapport puts the other person at ease, helping them to talk freely. You get to know them better, they like you more, and they're more likely to share their true thoughts and feelings. People with rapport often feel comfortable giving each other honest feedback and are more effective leaders. The proper rapport can also help you get new clients, friends, or a job interview; create a relaxed working environment, and even make you appear more attractive.

Learning how to build rapport is a skill that can be learned. You can listen actively, ask questions and take an interest in the other person by making statements based on what they tell you. Rapport takes practice, but it's worth it.

Rapport is built on the level of trust between two people. The more rapport you have, the deeper the trust. Understand that trust can be misplaced and fade rapidly when someone realizes they've been misled. Rapport is built by giving straightforward answers, being honest, and not promising anything you can't deliver. As a result, people will feel safe with you, contributing to their comfort level with your presence and ability to share feedback freely.

To make the most of rapport, you should know your audience and which types of people you're likely to encounter. Consider using the information you've gained to make an excellent first impression. Adapt your body language and tone of voice to the other person's demeanor. Use their words when asking questions and mirror their gestures, facial expressions, and gestures to create a connection with them.

Use the conversation as an opportunity to assess the other person. If they seem distracted or are avoiding eye contact, it might be because they don't like what they hear from you, or they see little or no value in what you have to offer them. In this case, you should listen to what they say and adjust your behavior accordingly. Don't be afraid to respond briefly and then move on unless they ask a question that requires you to elaborate.

The best way to know how someone will react is to watch them without coming across as too interested—don't be pushy or try too hard. The best way to find out about people is by asking questions and listening closely for the answers. This will help you find essential information about them, but only after the person has spoken. When you need more information, ask again later when the person is more relaxed or open. Your questions don't have to be complicated. A simple "How are you?" will have the other person speaking freely to you. You can ask follow-up questions such as, "What do you like best about your job?" Then listen attentively to their responses.

The best way to build rapport is by practicing with your family, friends, or anyone you care about. The next time someone brings a new person into the group—someone who seems shy or awkward—ask them about themselves and get them involved in the conversation immediately. The more experience you get, the easier it will be to build rapport with people at work or in your personal life.

Rapport is a vital communication skill that can be used not just to make others feel more comfortable but yourself. As you get to know the other person better and can build a strong relationship with them, they'll open up and be more forthcoming with their feelings and thoughts. This will help you see things from their perspective, judge their feelings or ideas, and make better decisions. With your newfound insight, you will then be able to connect with your customers or clients on a much deeper level than before.

Rapport is simple but complex. Building it takes practice and patience. It would be best if you worked at it and practiced often. The more you use it, the easier it will become. Understanding what's going on in a person's mind is difficult because many people are closed-minded and don't freely share their feelings. This can be because they feel threatened by someone who wants something from them or wants to keep their personal life private.

The best way to build rapport with people is by listening actively, paying attention, keeping your gestures and tone of voice appropriate for each individual, and then mirroring those gestures and body language when talking with them.

Benefits of building rapport.

- It increases your chances of getting what you want.

- It helps you get along better and be more productive at work.
- It improves your stress level by making you feel good.
- It makes new relationships easier to manage and grow.
- It can help you achieve more in less time because people will trust you more and be willing to listen when you speak.

Therefore, building rapport is essential to be successful in any business or personal relationship.

The first stage in building a rapport is adjusting our body language, facial expressions, and posture to the other person's demeanor. We need to make sure that we control our voices so that we do not lose control of our emotions, as this is a potent tool to have in our arsenal.

The second part of building a rapport with people is making them feel comfortable enough to open up and tell us how they think, their likes and dislikes, their hopes and dreams, and even the things they don't like so that we can get to the core of who they are. Since ancient times, people have used body language to build rapport with others. When you make that rapport, you're more likely to get what you want from them, and your communication becomes more effective. Therefore, adjusting your voice, body language, and posture to the other person makes it easier for them to open up and express themselves. Your body language is a potent tool in building that rapport.

The next part is about listening actively. You should begin by standing up and keeping your hands loose at your sides. You need to face the conversation and have good eye contact with the other person, not stare at them but look into their eyes and then turn your head away to increase the amount of time you look into them.

Networking
Networking is the process of introducing yourself to or building connections with people to explore opportunities for advancing your knowledge, professional skills, and career.

The primary benefit of networking is the opportunity to expand your network of contacts. In this instance, you obtain information, advice, or referrals that would otherwise likely be outside your contact's circle. Expanding your network also increases the likelihood of finding mentors and job opportunities. By boosting your social circle, you also expand your reach in many aspects of life and personal relationships.

There are many methods for networking. One of the most common is a combination of in-person, telephone, and online networking. Online and telephone networking are often used in conjunction with each other, while in-person meetings are used with phone and online meetings if necessary. People can choose to use any or all three methods to best suit their needs and schedule, but there is not one method that is more effective or productive than another.

Some advantages of expanding your network include the following:

- Allowing you to work on your own time.
- Promoting face time instead of phone time.

- Expanding your social circle.
- Making new professional connections (or maintaining old ones).
- Increasing your visibility and opportunities.
- Meeting new people involved in the same business or field as you.
- Gathering information and advice.
- Being able to make connections that have influenced those who matter most to your professional goals (people who have influence can be people who can help you get a job, advance in your career, or be more successful).

As you expand your network of contacts, you can discover a wealth of information and relationships that could benefit you in every area of life. Expanding your social circle, for instance, makes it easier to make new professional connections or maintain the ones you already have if necessary.

Networking is done by many people of all ages, including entrepreneurs, professionals, job seekers, and students. Whether you are looking to advance in your career or build a professional network for other reasons, networking is a great way to expand your circles and make new connections.

When networking, it is essential to focus on building relationships instead of only business transactions. People who focus just on business transactions tend to come across as insincere and uninterested in the relationship itself, which can end up closing doors instead of opening them.

This doesn't mean that you should always be the one giving the advice instead of taking advice from others; it means you should give without expecting anything in return. It would be best to focus on the relationship instead of solely on yourself. Your actions, such as providing advice to others, helping out with projects, and volunteering your skills, can help you gain their trust. It is also essential for you to maintain consistent contact with others in the networking community.

It would be best if you didn't overdo your networking to maintain a good image and professional contacts. To establish credibility and build a solid professional network, you must do many things that cannot be done over the phone or through email.

It is possible to network successfully in various ways:

- Make sure you maintain contact with those in your network by keeping in touch regularly through phone calls or e-mails.
- Put together a list of your contacts and the contacts' contact information.
- Make sure that you keep your list and contact information up-to-date so that it is easy for people to get in touch with you.
- Be sure to inform those around you about your network by introducing them to those you might have met who could help them.
- Use social media websites such as Facebook or Linkedin to connect with others.
- Put out a general call for new contacts through one or more professional networking sites, such as LinkedIn.

- Use networking groups to introduce yourself and make contacts in the business, social, or professional community.

Networking is a great way to get the support you need to advance your career. It can be one of the most rewarding things you do in your personal and professional life. As you begin networking, it is essential to remember that networking is all about building relationships with others. When making these relationships, you must take care of yourself and not burn bridges by being too pushy or obnoxious toward others.

Personalities and Forecasting Behavior

Communication is one of the most critical aspects of workplace success. Effective communication is also a significant factor in workplace relationships. Communication can often help build better relationships in the workplace, but it can also destroy those relationships daily. As human beings, we are not entirely alike, and we all have unique personalities. Many factors, such as family upbringing and childhood experiences, have shaped our personalities since birth. Personalities are a big part of how people view themselves and perceive others. Your personality also affects your communication style, which can significantly impact how others perceive you at and outside work.

The personalities of the people you work with can play a significant role in how you experience your relationships within the workplace. Over the years, four personality traits have been identified: conscientiousness, openness to experience, extraversion, and agreeableness. Openness to experience is a factor that is associated with curiosity, artistry, and tolerance. This trait also relates to abstract thinking, intellect, and knowing what makes you happy. Extraversion is marked by social skills and being outgoing in public situations or with others.

Extraverts are often self-confident and enthusiastic about their personalities and those around them. Other traits related to extraversion include talkative, assertive, and energetic behavior. Then there is agreeableness which is marked by a sense of being cooperative, kind, and helpful toward others. Agreeable people will tend to be polite and cooperative towards others, while they may not be as assertive or confident as people who are extroverts.

These personality traits can profoundly affect your workplace relationships, especially if they do not fit with the personalities of your co-workers. Certain personality traits, such as being highly conscientious, open to new experiences, and having weak social skills, will negatively impact your work performance. All of these traits can put you at risk for stress in the workplace.

Highly conscientious and conscientious people are generally of good character and do not need much hand-holding or assistance when learning new things. They will often be quick learners and prefer to work alone instead of working with others in the workplace. They also have a strong work ethic, which will often translate into being highly respectful towards the importance of the job that they are doing in the workplace. Therefore, creating a unique personality in the workplace is one of the most important factors to consider.

Being highly conscientious does not mean being a workaholic but merely being responsible and accountable for the way you manage your time. People who choose to be highly moral can quickly become stressed at work if no strategic plan is implemented for them. These individuals are hardworking and have exceptional skills in working towards personal goals.

Highly conscientious people can be easily bored if they do not have a plan of action laid out in front of them to work on. One of the best ways to keep motivated is by setting goals for yourself which will assist you in meeting those goals. Always include your co-workers in your goals since their ideas and assistance can help motivate you to complete those tasks with less effort or stress.

If you are working with a conscientious person in your workplace, try to delegate assignments and tasks that will help promote their growth at the job they have been assigned. If workers have questions about their duties or the task they are working on, they need to keep asking questions until all of the details have been worked out.

When dealing with highly conscientious people, you should keep meetings short. They may seem hesitant when it comes to meetings because they prefer to work independently from others instead of in groups or teams. This can be problematic since they will not be able to share their ideas and opinions with others, leading to an ineffective work relationship between you.

Chapter 6: The Foundations of Communication, the Forms It Takes, and the Elements That Comprise It

Communication is difficult. There are many ways to communicate, but we all know it's not as simple as learning a particular language and practicing. Communication is complex and vast. It requires much work, effort, and planning to get good at it.

What are the foundations of communication?

Foundations of communication are the techniques, skills, and behaviors used to convey one's thoughts, ideas, or emotions to another person. They are the things we learn and practice on a day-to-day basis to be good at communicating effectively. The foundation of communication is, first, how to listen; second, how to read someone's facial expressions; and third, how to speak or write about what's on your mind.

Listening

The first step in communication is listening. You can't communicate if you don't have a place you're talking from. One of the essential skills that are required for us to communicate effectively is the ability to listen. Listening isn't easy, but it's not impossible, either. It would be best to be attentive and alert to what people around you say or do. Being cautious and conservative will help you listen, but being present is key in communication. You must also be able to make yourself available, which means you have to be available when they need you. Being known is an essential skill in communicating effectively at any time.

You need to understand and put yourself in the other person's shoes before you can truly understand what they're trying to tell you. Additionally, you have to be able to take what the other person is saying and put it into your own words. Lastly, you have to remember your manners while listening. This includes staying quiet while they're talking, nodding when they're finished speaking, being respectful, etc.

Communicating effectively sometimes also means controlling how much we talk as well. It shouldn't be all about us, but rather a mutual exchange of ideas and understanding between two people. We should listen twice as much as we speak for our communication with each other to satisfy both parties involved.

Reading facial expressions

The second step in communication informs readers about what an individual thinks or feels by reading their facial expressions. The face is a tool that we all use to communicate with others. It's a potent tool, but it's also very misunderstood. Facial expressions are made up of muscles that surround the mouth, eyes, and nose. These muscles sometimes play tricks on us and misrepresent the feelings and thoughts that they're associated with. For example, when talking to someone, and their face becomes flushed red, many assume that the other person is angry or upset with them. However, there are many reasons for a flushed face, including temperature control (it could be hot in an office or other area), alcohol (if the person is drunk), embarrassment (if the person is ashamed about something), etc. If we wait to read the face and let our intuition kick in, we risk missing out on important things that someone is trying to tell us.

Reading a person's facial expressions is an essential skill to have to communicate effectively with different people. For us to be able to do this successfully, we need to be able to look at an individual's face and determine what it means. You have to put yourself in their shoes and think about it from their perspective before understanding what they're trying to tell you. Again, this requires being attentive and alert at all times, as well as keeping our minds open and understanding the possible emotions of another person.

Speaking or writing about what's on your mind

The third step of communication is all about communicating with others. The people around us can't read facial expressions but can read our minds. If we could share our thoughts and ideas through words, it would be up to other people to decide how we express ourselves. Again, this requires being always attentive and alert, but it also requires that we be able to express ourselves. Being able to express yourself is an important skill for communicating effectively. You must be able to speak and write clearly and coherently if you want others around you to understand what you're trying to say. To do this, we need patience with ourselves and to accept our mistakes from time to time. We should always strive to improve our writing and speaking skills, but if we try too hard or get frustrated, it can be the opposite of the result we're looking for.

Communicating effectively with others is essential to making our world a better place. Communication is vital in our everyday lives, but it's not easy. It requires a lot of work and effort to make it work, but being good at communicating can be very rewarding.

The forms that Communication takes

Communication can be formal or informal. A proper conversation requires a structure when two or more people are talking together. An informal conversation is used between two parties when they know each other well enough to understand how they will communicate.

- Formality: Formality is the level of formality of a communication situation. It influences how the result of communication will be perceived by those in attendance and those watching it on television.
- Informality: Informality is the level of informality or non-formalness in which communication occurs. This can be influenced by the situation, the audience, the formality of the situation, and the parties in communication.
- Formal vs. Informal: Formal is how language is structured; it is the standard language used in any communication situation involving two or more people. The informal nature of communication can be a significant factor influencing the outcome of communication. Informal conversation occurs between people who know each other very well and are comfortable sharing their thoughts, ideas, and feelings.

The elements that comprise communication
The following are communication elements and how they can be applied in various situations.
Five Elements of Communication:

1) Verbal and non-verbal communication: Verbal/Non-verbal communication occurs whenever an individual speaks and listens to another person verbally (words). Non-verbal communication occurs whenever an individual is not speaking or listening but can still communicate through touch, gesture, and body language. This means that non-verbal communication involves more than just the voice. It also requires attitude, posture, and movement.

2) Information exchange: The information exchange refers to the type of information being communicated, who it is from, and what it involves. The information exchanged or transmitted can be verbal (words), written (letters, e-mails, texts, etc.), or non-verbal. The information exchange can also be formal, informal, or formal and informal, depending on the situation. The type of information that is received from others is referred to as feedback.

3) Message: A message is any form of communication that you have given to someone else, either verbally (in person), written (via paper, email, or text), or non-verbally (body language). The sender sends out the message, and then it's received by the receiver. The receiver does not see what message was sent until they open it up and read it themselves. They will then interpret and understand the message, allowing them to respond. The response that they give can be verbal or non-verbal. It depends on how they interpret and understand what they read or hear. The answer can be agreement, support, dissent, or even confusion.

4) Feedback: Feedback is the response to the sender or individual who initially initiated the message. This is what determines how effective of a communicator you are. You should always listen to this feedback and take it at face value because it's an essential part of the communication process. Feedback should always be used to improve your communication skills.

5) Formal vs. Informal: The formal vs. informal communication element refers to the formality level at which a message is sent and received. The story of formality can be impacted by the situation, audience, and type of information being exchanged between individuals. Formal communication occurs when you communicate with someone you do not know well or have never met before. It also appears when you are communicating with someone who has power over you (e.g., manager, teacher, doctor, etc.) Informal communication takes place between people who know each other very well and can talk freely about anything they want to talk about at that moment. The informal nature of communication can be a significant factor influencing the outcome of communication.

Communication is essential in our everyday lives. It's up to us to take the time and effort to make sure that we are good at communicating with one another. It takes patience, tact, and a lot of practice, but being a good communicator will benefit you greatly in the future.

Be discreet and polite when communicating with others. The worst thing you can do is insult someone or make them feel bad while talking. Always be patient and listen carefully because communication is different for everyone, so it's essential not to take things personally when communicating with other people. Practice making small talk whenever you can. Whenever you go to a social or business event, get the opportunity to meet new people.

Chapter 7: The BIGGEST Mistakes People Make When Communicating

When communicating with people, we often do things that sabotage our communication efforts. When you do the following items, people get defensive and start to shut down and tune you out, which completely defeats the purpose of trying to communicate. But when you're in control of your own emotions and clearly understand other people's needs, you can become better at talking to anyone with anything.

You make errors in verbal communication. The common verbal communication errors that most of us make are as follows:

Mistake #1. You don't listen to what they're saying - when talking with someone, and you tend to take your thoughts and feelings hostage in the conversation instead of letting them speak. As a result, your mind starts wandering off into plans for the future or other ideas.

Mistake #2. You don't pick up their body language. They think you're not listening to them when you don't pick up on their body language. It's essential to read people's verbal and non-verbal communication.

Mistake #3. You don't clarify your thoughts. When speaking with someone, it's important to make sure that you know exactly what your intentions are - and you have to be very clear about your thoughts. Otherwise, the person won't know where their thoughts stand, which will cause them to start thinking about other things.

Mistake #4. You're not empathetic toward them. When you're not compassionate toward them, they feel they can't be open with you and share their honest thoughts and feelings. As a result, they shut down and tend to build up walls between themselves and others where they close off their true intentions.

Mistake #5. You don't have a solid understanding of their needs. When you don't have a strong knowledge of the person's needs, you don't know what to say or how to act when talking with them. You may end up saying something that completely offends them without realizing it.

When communicating with people, we often do things that sabotage our communication efforts. But when you're in control of your own emotions and clearly understand other people's needs, you can become better at talking to anyone with anything.

Mistake #6. You don't have a solid understanding of your own needs. When you don't understand your needs, you can develop feelings that cause a lot of tension in your body. As a result, when you're talking with someone, and things start getting emotional, you can lose control over your emotions and say something that might offend them or hurt their feelings.

Mistake #7. You're not aware of the other person's emotions. When you're not aware of the other person's emotions, it makes it difficult for them to explain what they feel to you because they can never develop the same awareness about their feelings in others around them. In a case like this, people tend to become defensive about their feelings because they don't fully understand them.

Mistake #8. You don't clearly understand what you want to achieve with them. When it comes to talking with someone, there are two primary goals we have to keep in mind:

a. Get them to open up and be aware of their feelings and thoughts.
b. To get them to be able to see us for who we are.
c. To do this, we have to have a solid understanding of our goals with others and how to talk in a way that persuades them toward those goals.

We need to make sure that we're making progress in our communication. We need to be coming from a place of wanting the other person's help and the best outcome possible, not just asking for something.

Mistake #9. This is one of the biggest mistakes we make when communicating with others. You don't clearly understand the outcome you're trying to achieve. The product should be beneficial for both parties. Otherwise, there's no real point in talking about it with them in the first place.

Mistake #10. You don't clearly understand how to communicate with people who are different from you. When you communicate with people who are different from yourself, you need to be aware that these people have another way of thinking and feeling about things than you do - and they may need more time to think out their decisions than those who are more in line with your way of thinking.

How can you best avoid these mistakes?
When communicating with anyone, you have to have a clear understanding of the following:

You have to be aware of what their needs are for you to understand how and where to communicate with them. You need to know how and where they're coming from so that you can share with them in a way that motivates them.

When your mind and body are relaxed, there's no resistance between you and other people - they can know what you want and how you want it from the start. When your mind is relaxed and in control of your emotions, nothing is holding back anything that wants to come out.

You need to know yourself very well so that you can understand what you want from people and how to communicate with them so that they can know what you want from them because then there's no confusion between the two of you.

You have to be aware of your own emotions to understand how other people are feeling and what they're communicating - and this is where we need to be empathetic toward everyone. You have to have a clear understanding of your own needs to know what your needs are - and this is where we need to ensure our needs only serve others.

We have to be aware of the outcome we're trying to achieve for us to know what it is we want from people. The product has to benefit everyone. Otherwise, there's no point in talking with them about it.

You need to know how to communicate with people who are different from you because other people have different ways of thinking and feeling about things than you do. You have to be conscious of this difference when talking with them for them to feel free and open with you.

Now that we've listed the mistakes people make when talking with others, let's review some key points about what to do instead.

Here are two basic guidelines for communicating with others:

a) People have different needs from you. When communicating with them, we must be aware of how they're feeling and think to understand how they are in their own world so that we can be there for them where they need us to be.

b) If you're going to be talking with someone, you need a clear understanding of what it is you want from them. It would be best if you had a clearly defined goal to achieve and communicated with them in a way that inspires action on their part toward those goals.

The mistakes people make when communicating with others result from not knowing how people think and feel, not knowing what their needs are, not understanding the outcome you want from them, and not being able to communicate with other people in a way that motivates them.

To communicate with others effectively, you need knowledge about what they need from you and an understanding of how they're communicating with you so that you can respond appropriately. To avoid these mistakes, we need to be constantly aware of each of these things. If we never get to practice and develop our communication skills, it's going to be very difficult for us to communicate with other people in a way that produces results.

Chapter 8: How to Read People and Connect With Different Personality Types

Whether you are trying to make friends, improve your relationship, or get people to do what you want - knowing how different personality types work and how to talk with them will help you immensely. Knowing how different personality types work is only half of the story. Like the weather, there is no one-size-fits-all approach to conversation. Every conversation is a little different. Every person you talk to will be different and have their preferences. And this means that you must be able to read people and connect with them individually.

The first thing to understand about talking with people is that you are not just talking to them - you are communicating with them. Every person is different, so every conversation will play out differently. Most people don't realize it, but you can tell almost everything about a person simply by paying attention.

Remember that every word you say has a specific purpose (to move the conversation forward) and that every emotion, reaction, or movement a person makes will contribute to how the conversation plays out. If you can learn to read people and their patterns, you can predict better what they will do next and how they will react.

People are hardwired to think in patterns. Once you understand people's patterns, you can predict how they will react in any given situation. Knowing how people work is helpful for many situations in life, as it helps us understand what motivates them and why we should do things a certain way. If someone wants something from you and it is not beneficial for you to give it to them, a specific thought pattern will occur inside their head. Knowing these patterns can help you avoid situations that are not beneficial for you or others.

Learning to read people and connect with them will make you far more successful in life, business, relationships, and even social environments such as parties or networking events. It will open up your communication skills to a new level and allow you to be much more confident in any situation. You can overcome situations using your personality and abilities if you know how people think. There are many different personality types, but they all follow the same models. People repeatedly use the same thinking patterns and feel confident they are right. But the fact is that they often aren't. They follow practices that have worked in similar situations and often miss seeing other options that could work better.

For example, if you want to be more charming, you will find out quickly that being overly serious will not help you at all. You need to connect with people, relax around them and make them feel comfortable enough to open up to you without feeling threatened by you (which is something many more serious people fail at). If you are serious and try to come off as some kind of authority figure, or a person that is better than others, you will find that people will not like you very much. If you want to be more charming and likable, on the other hand, you need to come off as friendly, open-minded, and understanding. You need people to feel comfortable around you - maybe even a bit vulnerable - because this will make them open up to you.

These "moves" work in almost any situation where people need to connect. More severe and formal people often find it challenging to make friends with those who are not like them. They will try to be friends in the relationship and expect the other person to come around their way of thinking. The problem is that people have a hard time doing this, so they end up alone most of the time. If you can learn how personality types work, you will find many ways to communicate with others and build connections that benefit everyone involved.

People Problems

Personality types tend to conflict because we all want different things out of each situation. Many people out there want to fit in and be popular. Still, they tend to get along better with people who are more like them instead of those who are different. This can cause a whole lot of problems for those who are in their group, especially when the person ends up getting negative attention from those who are not in their group.

If your goal is to build relationships with groups of adults and younger people, it is good to find out how much you will clash with various personality types. For example, those who have a more severe personality will often fight with those whose characters are more laid-back and fun-loving. These differences will cause conflict because neither person is willing to change their side of the argument. For example, if you are a more serious person trying to build friendships with fun and outgoing people, you will often feel alienated. These people like to party, hang out and have a good time. On the other hand, you might be looking for something more serious and meaningful. You want to find someone to talk deeply about things with and connect with on a deeper level.

The other person might go along but be upset inside because they didn't see things the same way as you. The best thing you can do is try to understand that they see things differently from you so that they will react differently. This means that you need to act in a way that is consistent with how they see things so that they will be as comfortable with you as possible.

More serious people react negatively when others do not act as expected. This can happen when there is a disagreement between two groups of people, or it can be something that occurs between just two individuals. For example, if you are a more serious person and you start talking to someone fun-loving, they might not take you as seriously as you would like them to. This can make you feel isolated or that your concerns do not matter to the other person. This can also manifest itself in people being moody and unpredictable.

It would be best if you built a connection with the other person by connecting on their level - something often difficult for more serious people because they don't want to let go of the need for it all to make sense. In this case, you must stop behaving in a severe manner around them and begin acting as they would expect from someone who does not take things too seriously. However, if you can learn to recognize the differences in how people think, you will be able to connect with them on a deeper level, build a connection and have a lot more fun in your conversations.

This is one example of how people may act differently depending on who they are with. It is always essential to understand that others see things from their perspective, however much we might disagree with it. By understanding this basic fact about human nature and how personalities work, you will be able to build better connections with others so that everyone feels comfortable around each other.

There are ways to improve your conversational skills and get the person you are talking to comfortable:

1) Always be positive, even if you are criticizing

When you criticize someone, they will often feel defensive. They will not want to listen to what you say and will not be happy. Instead of attacking directly, try being positive and avoiding criticism. If you want someone to do something and they aren't doing it right or the right way, explain how you would like it done or suggest how you think it should be done. By doing so, the person you are talking with will have much less chance of feeling defensiveness and will be more likely to change their behavior to be closer to what you would like.

2) Build trust with everyone you talk to

Trust is a big part of communication. People are different, and so the way that you build trust with someone will be further from the person beside you. When talking to someone, try to find common ground or something that you both have in common. For example: If you are trying to get your partner to move into another apartment, try asking them about when they had to move and what made it difficult for them (common ground). People feel more comfortable when they can relate things in their past to things happening around them now. Building trust with people can simultaneously achieve more of what you want and what they want.

3) Take the time to listen to people

This one is a little harder. If you are trying to talk with someone, but they are not talking back, or they are talking about something that has nothing to do with you, ask the person what is in their mind. Listen and pay attention! This can be hard because, often, people do not want to be interrupted when they are talking. But by asking what is going on in their minds, you will learn a lot about them and be able to connect with them better.

4) Use core values/interests as a guide

When you know who someone is and where their interests lie, you will find it easier to understand their personality type and how they think. When you know this, you can use it to explain yourself and connect with them better. For example, if you are an artist and someone else knows, they will be more likely to listen to your advice and share their views. If you are talking with someone who shares the same interests, it is good to try connecting their interests with something important in your life now. When you connect people's core values with what is essential in your life, it helps them feel like they are more involved and interested in what is happening around them.

5) Use body language to your advantage

Keep track of everything you do with friends, family, and loved ones. Pay attention to how they sit, stand, or move and use this information. Often people will not notice when you are doing something slightly different (for example, not leaning on their desk as much), but over time this small thing will become more prominent. People have practiced sitting and standing in certain ways for years leading up to the specific situations they are in now. But what might be essential for them might not be very important for you and vice versa.

6) Understand the need for status

People want to feel important. Understanding this makes it easier to connect and become involved with others. For example, group members (such as team members, club members, or family) will want to feel like they are essential. They will want people to think that they are "in the know" and know what is happening in the group. People struggling socially and in life will often overcompensate by trying to impress others or create status by creating the illusion that they know more than they do. By understanding how groups (whether it be family members or friends) work, you can better distinguish whether someone is truly important or not.

7) Do not take things personally

Most people take things personally. They will see what you say (even if you realize that it is not a personal attack), and they will instantly begin to think about themselves, whether the thing you are talking about is good or bad for them. This can be highly frustrating for individuals who want to connect with others but cannot because of this. If people comment negatively on something that does not affect them, try to understand why they are saying it. You need to be able to find the reason behind their behavior; this will make it easier for you to connect with other people and increase your relationships.

Why People React Differently To Each Other

To communicate better with others, you need to understand their personalities. How someone sees the world is different from how another person sees it. This is caused by how people think; these differences affect their feelings. You can connect with people more personally and increase your relationships by understanding how people think. When you do this, you will understand people better and avoid the mistakes that most people make. You will also be able to express yourself and connect with others more effectively. By understanding other people's personalities, you can communicate with people better and build your relationships.

Human beings are hardwired to be sociable creatures. We all have specific patterns ingrained into us, so we can function in specific ways in a particular environment. However, it is not always easy to understand how people think or what motivates them when they make decisions and engage in situations they disagree with. By learning about these patterns, we can begin to understand people better and show them that our opinions matter. When we think about other people's needs before ourselves, our relationships become much more effective. We can also begin to read other people's body language and understand their motivations better. Paying attention to what people are doing and listening to what they have to say will help you connect with them and have a much more effective conversation.

Realize that all people are different, and we all have different ways of thinking about the world. Knowing how people feel is essential to understanding others, but it is not something that you should try too hard to develop or master. So, take a moment to discover what personality type you fall into and build connections with people based on that personality. The benefits of this are huge. Follow these tips on connecting with others, and you will improve your ability to communicate more effectively in any situation, regardless of your personality type.

Chapter 9: The Invisible Barriers Against Effective Communication and How to Address Them

It's hard to imagine how many barriers exist between two people in different places with different paths. They might be friends, colleagues, business partners, strangers on the street, etc., and they might want to talk to or even connect. Yet, there are always invisible barriers in the way, and then we wonder why it is so hard to secure. It's like two people who want to say something important but, for some reason, can't find a commonly spoken language. They might want to, but they don't know how. This book focuses on the communication barriers you face when you need to talk to someone at the moment and how to deal with them.

What are the barriers to effective communication?

There are many barriers to effective communication, yet there is one that stops most people from even trying to communicate. They cannot say what they want in a way others can hear or understand. It's like a linguistic disability that can be defined as communication anxiety. It's a feeling of vulnerability and uncertainty about approaching others, getting their attention, and then delivering the message for them to understand what you want.

You might think something wrong with your personality makes you anxious about communication, but this isn't true. If you have such feelings often, it's no surprise you struggle with communication daily. It's not you responsible for that feeling, but the way society has been built and conditioned. We live in a society where people are afraid to communicate directly and openly. That's why we use words so sparsely and often don't know how to say what we want to say clearly.

Some of the invisible barriers against effective communication include:

1. The tendency to lose your identity in the crowd: For example, someone addresses a large group simultaneously, and no one knows who they are talking about. It's easy for people to lose their identity when they communicate with many different people at once in the same room. People's identities (elements of themselves or personas) shift between interactions with other people, and therefore they have little chance of knowing what they want and implementing it. This can be a problem at work where people can't say what they want because they are afraid of conflict, looking bad, or being wrong. This deficiency in communication skills is likely to lead to problems.

2. You are expected to take the initiative, and then you don't: We have many situations like that, where you need to initiate a conversation or strike the first word, but you don't. For example, someone is sitting on a park bench alone reading a book, standing in line at the supermarket alone, or waiting at the bus stop alone. It might seem as if no one wants to engage in a conversation but think about it for a minute. Does it make sense? We are all social creatures who seek out interactions with others to grow as individuals. We are all pretty much the same. We all want to connect with others for 5 minutes or forever.

3. You are afraid of revealing too much about yourself: Sometimes, we are scared to reveal our true selves because it might be considered offensive. For example, we tell others who we are, what we want, and what motivates us. We are scared of being criticized, scolded, or judged by others. So instead of talking to somebody like a person, we usually try to hide our real intentions and thoughts about ourselves in order not to get rejected or hurt. We fear what people might think of us if they know our thoughts and intentions. It's easier to keep people at a distance by not being too honest and direct about ourselves. Instead, we are expected to present ourselves in less than our usual selves. When we do that, it's hard to form a connection with others.

4. We don't know how to be vulnerable: To admit your weakness and ask for help is the most important thing you can do when you want to connect with people you care about or regularly interact with. It's like the root of communication, the start of all communication. You can learn it from many places such as psychology, sociology, or even just observing other people, for example, when playing sports, playing guitar, or dancing. It's just that many people don't know how to use it helpful when talking to others. It's like our mother nature. We are all vulnerable from the moment we are born into this world and spend all our time learning how to be vulnerable, no matter our race, culture, or background.

5. Fear of conflict: This might be the most significant barrier to effective communication because people fear confrontation and argument. They want to say something but are afraid they won't find the right words, or they will get angry or even say something stupid in front of other people. Therefore, they prefer not to talk about important issues rather than say something wrong. That's why it is essential to include tactical communication skills in your communication toolkit.

6. The lack of confidence: People are afraid to speak up and share their opinion because they don't feel confident enough and think that what they say might not be suitable or interesting enough. They believe others will judge them if they say something wrong, stupid or irrelevant. That's why you need to know what makes people interested in your opinions and how you can deliver them in a way that people want to listen to and understand rather than criticize you.

7. Lack of interest: This is another barrier people face when trying to communicate with others. People don't want to talk about things that are not important or interesting enough, be it their problems, work problems, or anything else. This is why you need to learn how to remove barriers and make meaningful and valuable communication for others in your communication skills training.

What stops you from communicating effectively?

Our society has been built because we are taught to be shy and avoid conflict. It's not how we were brought up but how we have been conditioned into thinking. In some cases, fear can be used as a good sense of self-protection against potential risks. So instead of being open and honest with others, we prefer to stay quiet, and everyone will know what we want without having to tell them or say it out loud. In other situations, however, fear can be used against us to control our lives. Conflicts can be used as threats to keep us in a lower position in the hierarchy, in which case we are used to thinking we can't do anything about it but just take the punishment and suffer silently. If we don't get what we want because someone is blocking it, then that's a good time to start taking things into your own hands rather than being passive. We are just as good as anyone else, so you deserve to get what you want and need.

If we cannot be ourselves, there is no point in trying to connect with others. We are not the same people we were born with; we grow and change during our lifetime. Therefore, we must accept the person we have become and dwell within that person rather than trying to be someone else. The only way of communicating effectively is to be fully present in the moment and not worry about what other people might think of you. Why would you worry about that anyway? It would be best if you only cared about how well or poorly a conversation goes on with another human being.

The way you communicate makes you look at yourself and others differently. It's like a layer of glass standing between yourself and others, so you cannot perceive what is happening. Sometimes you need to look through that glass to see the accurate picture and understand how others see it.

The most important thing you can learn in communication is how to listen to other people, not just for understanding but for the ability to communicate with them. Does this sound too simple? It's like understanding yourself better. You can only understand others if you can understand yourself first. So when you say things out loud, you need to be aware of what you are saying by noticing your behavior, body language and words, and other people's emotions. Otherwise, you won't be able to achieve what you set out for in your communication training.

How do you overcome the invisible barriers against effective communication?

This is the only question we will focus on in this book because it's the most fundamental problem people face when they try to communicate with others. No magic pill you can take will automatically remove the barriers and make you an effective communicator. Communication is something you learn and practice over and over again. The good news is that once you know how to communicate effectively, it will stay with you forever, and you will use your communication skills daily.

You will also be able to improve your communication skills by learning how to overcome the barriers that block and prevent effective communication.

Here are tips on how to overcome the invisible barriers to effective communication:

How do we overcome problems in communication?

First of all, you need to learn how other people communicate. If you are interested in someone else, the chances are you will become good friends if you can understand them, what makes them tick and what motivates them. Why is that so? It's because understanding someone else helps build trust between two people. The more faith there is between two people, the easier it will be for two people to connect and form a meaningful relationship or, in other words, a friendship that lasts forever.

1. Tune into your own emotions: If you don't know how you feel, how can you expect to read the feelings of others? It's essential to be self-aware and learn how to communicate with yourself calmly so you can then communicate with other people calmly.

2. Be present in the moment: You cannot communicate effectively if your mind is elsewhere. You need to be fully there and focus on what's happening, who's around, and what they are saying so that you can respond to their needs rather than your own. This also applies when you talk on the phone or speak face-to-face with someone.

3. Don't be afraid to ask questions: To understand someone, you need to know what they want, which means asking them. This can be awkward and difficult at first, but it's an absolute must for effective communication. You need to make sure that you listen thoroughly, are interested in what the other person has to say, and don't rush through the conversation so you can get away from uncomfortable situations or people as quickly as possible.

4. Confidence is critical: Confidence is part of how people communicate, interact with others, and feel about themselves in life. Your communication skills training will show if you don't feel confident about yourself. If you are optimistic, others will instantly be attracted to you and want to talk with you. It's essential to put yourself out there and start being more spontaneous. The more confident and relaxed you become, your communication skills training will be more effective.

5. Be aware of what you want to talk about: Before you start the conversation, think about what the other person has to say and what you would like to ask them. If you don't know what to say, see if you can come up with an idea before starting a conversation. Also, try to learn more about the person from their words and body language before speaking to understand that person better.

6. Accepting your emotions: One of the best ways to improve communication is to start accepting yourself. This means being in a good mood, buying all your feelings, and knowing you are good enough to communicate with others.

7. Don't let fear block you: If someone is blocking you from achieving something you want, let go of the fear so you can move forward and complete it yourself. Get rid of everything that stands in your way, learn how to manage life situations on your own, and manage things so that they work out for the better.

8. Learn to listen: It's not just important to hear what people say; learning how to listen makes others feel better because they feel you care. You will also be able to communicate with them more effectively if you show that you are listening.

9. Don't take things personally: If someone is angry or upset, they haven't done it just because of you. People have their own lives and problems, so don't blame yourself for being unable to fix them or solve the problem for them. Take things as they are and work on improving your communication skills training.

10. Flexibility is vital: If people want to communicate in a certain way, you should go along with it. If the other person wants to be more serious, then do that. If the other person wants to lighten the mood and be happy, follow suit and become satisfied. It's all about being flexible.

Communication is about being transparent, open, and honest with each other. Invisible communication barriers can be compared to blocks that prevent people from connecting, communicating, and working together. These barriers are hidden, but they are very much there. If you want to communicate effectively with others, try to eliminate the barriers to communication by listening, understanding, and respecting others. You will see the results of your communication skills training. Also, keep in mind the tips that have been mentioned in this book on how to overcome invisible communication barriers. This will help you communicate better with others and in life and develop a better personal relationship with yourself.

Chapter 10: Secrets to Becoming an Empathetic Listener and Conversationalist

If you have difficulties establishing and maintaining relationships within any circle, the lack of communication skills is probably one of the reasons. It is essential to effectively communicate your thoughts and ideas, not only to you but also to other people. Speaking skills are the starting point of any relationship. From a young age, we are all taught that communication is essential and it is something that you will always have with you. The problem, however, with many people is that they forget how important and valuable it can be to them and others, especially when they are in a relationship with another person or even someone at work.

Communication is something that you're always supposed to be able to achieve. Whether you are talking to your friends, family members, a girlfriend or boyfriend, or even when it comes to communicating at work or school, communication is essential, and something that you should always be able to have with every single person in your life, why do we forget about it and why do we have issues when it comes to relationships? Many of us are too afraid of hurting the other person's feelings or becoming awkward in some way by not being able to communicate well with the people we love or even with those we work with.

So if communication is essential for every aspect of your life, why do so many people forget about it and let relationships fall apart because they cannot communicate? The answer to this question is quite simple—we all want to be liked and accepted by everyone. We want everyone to get and love us just the way we are, with no faults and imperfections. We need to be taken by others to feel safe and secure. However, we also tend to be too judgmental towards people around us. Many of us tend to forget that everyone is different from one another, whether it's their personality or simply the way they look at life.

Because we want people to like us for who we are and don't want them to point out our faults or imperfections, we forget how essential communication skills can be for our relationships. We want to be like everyone else, and by communicating with others, we can better understand them and get to know them on a more personal level. By communicating well with someone, we can tell them about ourselves, let them tell us about themselves, and learn more about that particular person. If we don't communicate well with someone and don't take the time to listen, we will never really know who they are or what they think or feel. And if we don't know someone very well, then they will be just another person to us. We will see them as strangers, cats, or dogs. Someone we don't know and someone who doesn't matter to us.

Communication is the starting point for every relationship that you might have in your life. We need to be able to listen and talk with people for relationships to work with each other. If you are unable to communicate well with someone, then you won't be able to understand them, and that relationship won't last very long at all.

From the time we learn to speak, we also know how to listen; but in some cases, this does not seem to be taught or practiced enough. Most people listen to what others say, but rarely can they make sense of the conversation, let alone respond appropriately. In a relationship, this lack of empathy and ability to be understanding is seen as a sign of disrespect. It is often considered when deciding whether you can be in a relationship with someone.

So what are the secrets to becoming an empathetic listener and conversationalist?

1. Commit to listen

Listen to others. Sometimes you want others to listen to what you have to say, but these people may not be able to pay attention to what you're saying. If this is the case, then use this time as an opportunity to learn from them. Listen and learn from their experiences because, in a way, they are also teaching you how not to have the same life as theirs. It's about giving and receiving; nothing is without effort, so giving worth listening to will give you some suitable lessons.

2. Always have a genuine interest in what others say

Genuine interest doesn't always mean you agree with their perspective, but it does mean that you are open to listening and learning from them. If you don't seem genuinely interested in what they have to say, they will feel ignored and frustrated with you.

3. Show interest by asking questions

Ask questions if you or someone else is expressing a point of view. A good way of asking questions is to keep the exchange from becoming one-sided by asking for further information about what the other person is saying. The more specific your question is, the more likely you'll get an answer, and that answer should lead to another question where possible.

4. Make sure you are giving them your full attention

If you are busy and in a hurry, don't ask the other person to listen to what you have to say. You have to lead by example regarding things like empathy and listening. People will not only learn communication skills from you, but they'll also pick up on your attitude. You can't expect others to attend if you are never willing or able to give the same respect in return.

5. Don't make assumptions about what you hear

You must be very careful when making assumptions about what you hear. We tend to believe that the first words out of someone's mouth are always accurate. This is not always the case because people don't always communicate as they want. When you listen, ask questions, and remember that people always try to tell you something. Sometimes they may have a point different from your own, but they will still reach an agreement or a compromise with the other person if they see that it is worth persevering with.

6. Don't interrupt

The art of listening is unique; sometimes, it requires you to be patient with the speaker. If they choose to speak, continue to listen; you cannot make it your business to speed things up or hurry them along. You must listen with your full attention and

allow others to talk or express themselves. The essential part of communication is hearing the other person, not only what they are saying but also their feelings at that particular time.

7. Don't make judgments

The art of listening is a potent tool to have. It can help you to understand someone's perspective and get insight into their message. The problem is that when people are bent on making judgments, they often miss the point the speaker is trying to convey. The art of listening requires you to show genuine interest in what others have to say, regardless of whether or not you agree with it or would like them to say something more specific. Judgments are made because we feel we can do things better than others. The art of listening allows you to open yourself up to a different perspective, which you may find surprising or even enlightening.

8. Give people feedback

The art of good communication is simply being able to hear not only what someone says but also hearing them. Don't be afraid to tell the other person what you think about what they say. If it is positive, compliment them. If it is negative, let them know. If a person is telling you that they cannot receive information from someone else in a certain way, let them know; this will allow you to find ways for this problem to be resolved and perhaps resolve it before it even comes up.

Communication is a powerful thing. It can provide us with some fantastic opportunities and experiences. Communication works both ways; you will find that whatever you put into the universe, positive or negative, will always come back to you. The same goes for communication; if you want to be someone others trust and feel comfortable telling about their problems or life experiences, you have to do the same for them when they open up to you. If we send out specific signals or clues that we are unwilling to listen to, people will close themselves off us. This means they will stop sharing their ideas and feelings with us because they feel they cannot trust us enough to listen without judgment or interruption. It is not always easy to be a good listener, but it can be one of the most rewarding things that you ever learn to do. Don't waste your chance and learn to listen more, for it will make all the difference in your relationships.

Being an empathetic listener means listening to the intent and message of the other person. It means being respectful in what you say, your voice, and your facial expressions. It also means focusing on the person's needs, wants, desires, and goals. A good listener is available to take in what they have to say, ask questions when necessary and let them know that you are interested in hearing from them. They will feel accepted, valued, and seen by the other person. Being an empathetic listener is not just about words but about showing people that you care for them personally and professionally.

It takes time and effort to be a good listener. It is not something that can easily be accomplished overnight. The art of listening is not just about hearing another person's words but also about hearing the intention behind those words. Good listeners will take their time to understand what the other person is trying to tell them. They make sure they truly understand the message, no matter how difficult or uncomfortable it may seem at first. It doesn't matter how long it takes to comprehend what someone is trying to say fully; they will do whatever they need to understand the message correctly.

Being an empathetic listener means putting the other person first. It doesn't matter what the other person is saying or how they are saying it. All that matters is that their needs and desires are being met. Their feelings are more important than your own; it doesn't matter what you want, as long as you can help them to get what they need. The art of listening requires a willingness to accept someone else for who they are, faults and all, without judging who they should be or should have been in the past.

A good listener is open and non-judgmental to all communication from others. They don't jump to conclusions and try to remain calm and relaxed when communicating. They don't judge what others say or how they say it. They take in other people's feelings and thoughts without being defensive or hurt. A good listener is interested in learning what another person has to say, who they are, and their hopes, dreams, aspirations, and goals.

Patience and understanding of human nature are part of the art of listening. It takes time to develop the ability to listen well. The art of listening requires a willingness to give your full attention to the person you are talking with. It means learning how their mind works, taking in what they have just said, and seeing all the emotions that may be guiding them in their actions and expressing themselves. It also means being able to listen to unspoken messages as well as what is being said.

It takes two people for communication to work. However, it does not mean you will automatically be a good listener. You will need someone willing to let you know what they want and allow you to understand where their thoughts and feelings are coming from. A person that can give you feedback so that you can learn what they think and feel when it comes down to communicating with others. It would be best if you had someone who has confidence in your ability so that they can fully express themselves without worrying about being misunderstood or misinterpreted by others. A good listener makes sure the other person understands what they are trying to say, even if it is difficult or painful for them. They give their honesty and genuine concerns so that they know they care and it is not a waste of their time when talking to them. This also shows they want to understand who they are as an individual. A good listener is willing to listen to what the other person has to say and how they say it and ask for clarification when necessary.

Being a good listener means listening and finding out what the other person wants and needs from you. It means understanding their goals as well as giving them the ability to express themselves and their feelings. It also means being aware of what the other person is feeling. They are not just reacting out of fear or anger; there may be more. They feel something else but aren't sure what they are doing, thinking, and feeling at that moment. A good listener will discover this to understand better and support their partner no matter what is causing them discomfort or pain in their lives.

Chapter 11: How to Form Your Message to Get Your Point Across Effectively

Have you ever been confused about how to start a conversation with someone? If you have, you've probably missed out on potentially great discussions. Imagine that you want to talk to someone, and they are not giving you eye contact or seem disinterested in talking. You might feel unwelcome and think it is difficult for them to stand there and listen to your story. Or you might be talking to an individual and wonder if you should tell them about the latest movie or book you just read.

Think about a time when someone didn't give you eye contact or when their responses seemed slow. What was their response to your comments? Was their body language helpful? If not, how did they respond?

Remember how they responded, and then use this knowledge in future conversations to help you maintain a relationship with that person. The next time a good friend or family member comes up to talk to you, consider what approach worked best for that person in your current situation. Did you make an interesting comment? Did you tell them a joke? How could you improve your approach and make their next visit more fun or meaningful?

What are some common mistakes people make while communicating with other people? What do some people do in their conversations that help to drive away listeners or create an awkward situation?

We all experience communication problems at some point in our lives. Even if we have developed excellent communication skills, sometimes people will not always understand us the way we want them to. Communication is a two-way street, so we must ensure that both parties understand one another.

Here are some helpful tips on how to form your message to get your point across effectively:

1) Ask for clarification if you want a second chance at conveying your point: The first thing that comes to mind when thinking of asking someone for clarification is a student who asks their teacher the same question repeatedly. It doesn't matter how often you ask this person; they will not remember what you said or how to answer your questions. Even if you are talking about something simple like "When did Ike become president?" and ask them several times for clarification, they might still have no idea what happened.

2) Stick with one topic: When in a conversation, sit back, relax and listen to the other person's responses. Do they respond to your comments with enthusiasm? If so, you're in a good spot. Don't press the matter if their body language is unfriendly, defensive, or uninterested. The more you try to get their attention and demand your point, the less receptive they will be to what you are saying.

3) Let them know what you want from them: "I want to talk to you about something that can make a big difference in our lives." This shows your listener that you have at least one topic in mind and asks for their input. It also lets them know that it is essential to you.

4) Listen to the other person: People who value conversation will find a way to make all the people they talk to feel comfortable. Pay attention to their words if you are interested in what they say. If you are only concerned with getting your points across, it will be challenging to know what they want or how their thoughts might influence yours. This can ruin a good relationship because friends and family don't like feeling that their space is being invaded by someone else and are pushing for you to go away.

5) Know how to say "no" (without coming across as rude): Learn how to say "no" as soon as you realize that the topic might not be exciting or pertinent for the circumstances and people around you. The purpose of saying "no" is to let them know it is not a good time for that topic and help them to move on with something that might work better.

6) Prepare what you want to say: What can you say that will be meaningful and engaging? You might not even get what you wanted to say out in the first place. It is best to have a few prepared lines or ideas before you start to speak. If you have nothing prepared, then you can easily fall into a meandering conversation that lasts longer than it should.

7) Know when to pause and let the other person talk: You might want to respond to what the other person says, but you are obligated to listen first. Sometimes this means you need a little bit of time so that you can form your thoughts and comments. Don't be in a hurry when it comes to starting your thoughts. Give yourself as much time as necessary, especially if the other person is talking fast or it seems like they are rushing through their words.

8) Avoid interrupting: The simple rule is that if someone's comments are confusing you or seem out of place, let them have a chance to present their thoughts before you jump in with your questions or comments. People appreciate it when someone takes their time to think about what they want to say, has patience, and tries not to interrupt them when they say something important.

9) Take notice of how you say something: There are two parts to the message you are sending. The first part is what you're saying, and the second is how you say it. This can mean your body language and tone of voice. You want to ensure that what you say matches up with your tone of voice or body language. If someone seems upset, ensure that your message matches the style of their voice or body language style. If someone seems happy, ensure your message matches their facial expressions and overall mood.

10) Maintain eye contact: Often, people will not speak with us unless we maintain eye contact. They might even tell us to look away if they are uncomfortable looking at someone. When trying to convey something to another person, there is no need to avoid their gaze and stare at the ground or the middle of their face. Stay focused on their eyes and maintain an appropriate level of eye contact.

11) Be truthful: You cannot be dishonest and expect a good result from your conversation. If you lie, it will likely come across in your voice tone or body language, making the person feel more uneasy with you than if you were honest from the start. Honest and open communication is the best way to maintain a good relationship with others.

12) Avoid being judgmental: No one wants to be judged by their opinions, thoughts, and feelings. If you think someone is wrong or their view is too romantic, it is best to think about how you want to respond. The best way of responding could be just saying, "I understand where you are coming from, but I want to let you know that I disagree." You could also say, "I disagree with that thought because of this reason. " Try not to judge what they say or paraphrase what they believe in a way they find offensive. If you can't do this, it will be better to keep your thoughts to yourself and not get into a long, drawn-out explanation of why they are wrong.

13) Use the person's name: This shows that you have an interest in who they are as a person. You can also use their name in your comments or responses to let them know you are paying attention to what they are saying. You don't have to say their word in every other sentence, but make sure you throw in some references that respect the other person's identity.

14) Avoid multitasking when you are in a conversation: Be present and focused on the other person. You might have stuff going on in your life, but you have to set them aside for the time being to have an intimate and meaningful relationship with the person you are speaking to. If you choose to act like there is something more important than talking to someone, don't be surprised if they seem upset or offended by what you are saying. They don't let these things slide because they want a good relationship with somebody who cares about them.

Getting your point across effectively can be tough every time you try. There are some instances where you might have to say the same thing repeatedly to get your point across. If you can learn how to do this effectively, it could mean that people might start noticing who you are and what you have to say. You could become a compelling individual because of how you communicate with others.

When speaking, try to find ways to make your communication more personal and meaningful by being truthful and exhibiting integrity at every opportunity. You want everyone to know that you care about them as a person and not just as an object used for your gain or pleasure unless it is part of a consensual relationship.

As you get older and deal with more people, you might learn that being an effective communicator will help ensure you live a fulfilling life and have a good relationship with others. You don't have to be an eloquent speaker to be able to say what needs to be said effectively.

It will take time, but if you are persistent and patient, you can learn how to become an effective communicator. You'll be surprised by the amount of positive feedback from communicating effectively. When other people see this happening, they will want to get involved in communication because they see how fruitful it is for your social relationships.

With communication, you must be open to feedback, criticism, and the possibility of being wrong. You will be wrong sometimes, but that doesn't mean that your alternative perspectives aren't valid. It would be best to consider other options before deciding what's more sensible or plausible.

When you are open to a good conversation and willing to respect the other person's point of view, they are likely to listen and believe what you have to say. They might not always agree with your point of view, but they will at least listen intently so as not to miss anything important that you might say.

The more you learn to be a good communicator, the more people will say positive things about you. Effective communication allows you to stand out from the crowd and attract people by demonstrating your commitment to being an effective communicator.

As an effective communicator, you are someone that other people can depend on because they know you are trustworthy and reliable. You can help others when they need it most because they can be assured that you will listen intently and provide what is required. They know your advice is worth considering, even if it isn't always followed. The other person will probably feel that whatever you say is important enough to understand and listen to.

As you become a more effective communicator, new relationships can blossom and grow in your life. Your friends, family, and acquaintances will notice your growth in this area and see you as someone they can be comfortable being around. You'll have a way of communicating that encourages others to be open with you, which means you are more likely to be motivated and inspired daily.

Finding out how important effective communication is in a relationship might make you want to do things differently. You will get your point across effectively so that the other person knows that you are sincere and have their best interest in mind. You will be interested in learning how they are doing daily and be mean to make sure they know you care about them as more than just a friend or acquaintance. When you learn how to be an effective communicator, it will open up whole new horizons for you. You'll be able to focus on having meaningful and intimate relationships with the people around you. You'll also know that whenever you want to talk about something important, someone will be willing to listen intently and show their support for what is being said. With effective communication, you can create an atmosphere where others can hear what you have to say and take it into account when making decisions. You'll find that others will come to you when they want a thoughtful perspective on a situation, so make sure you are always ready to give your two cents. If all else fails, keep telling them the same thing differently until they understand what you are trying to say.

Chapter 12: The Art of Conveying Your Thoughts and Feelings Across Different Mediums

Have you ever found yourself in a scenario where you've been told to do something but don't know how and find it extremely difficult to communicate that fact? The person you're speaking to isn't making it easy on themselves, either. Perhaps they feel the same way that they aren't being heard or might be in a situation where they don't want their feelings hurt.

Well, it's no surprise that communication skills are so integral - our jobs rely on us being able to articulate ideas clearly and concisely. Yet it's astonishing how many of us don't know how best to do this. Understanding another person's tone of voice and body language is essential to convey your message. When we have a conversation, our tone, choice of words, and body language can tell the other person whether we're being friendly or hostile towards them.

Communicating your thoughts and feelings across different mediums, especially during a conversation, is extremely important, but there are two parts you need to get right:

First, you need to read the person you're speaking to and ensure they're in an excellent mental and emotional place to talk. We do this by observing their body language and tone of voice. This will give the impression that you care about the other person's well-being.

Your tone of voice is vital for communication consistency with what you're saying. If you're speaking in a monotone voice or sounding disinterested, the other person will get bored or not take you seriously.

Secondly, as you begin to talk about this issue/topic, think about what the other person needs to hear and how you can show them by example. The best way to do this is through stories. When we tell stories, we use words that excite our emotions and paint a picture in others' minds. Most of us don't like to be told that we're boring or that our stories are boring, so it's essential to paint a picture and give examples that will make your story interesting.

Many people are afraid to talk in groups because they think they're not good enough or will say the wrong thing. Once you understand your communication skills, you won't have to worry about this! If you feel uncomfortable talking in front of a group, try practicing in front of a mirror or with friends and family. You can start practicing on others when you get used to it and feel more confident. Remember that if you want people to listen to your opinion/proposal, make sure it's short and snappy. Don't beat around the bush - get straight to the point.

If you're in the middle of a conversation and feel like you're not being listened to, stop speaking, look away from the other person, and think about how you can be more direct. This will make your message more understandable for them.

This will only work if it's done respectfully. If you've rolled your eyes or scoffed at what they've said, they'll take it as a sign that you don't care or that they should take a break so their feelings won't hurt. Remember, you're initiating the conversation, and it's not your job to correct people constantly. If you're trying to convince someone of something, then you have a responsibility to get them on board with what you're saying.

Another way you can improve your communication skills is to see if the other person is getting bored. If they are, repeat what they've said using different words or tell them how you feel about it. People will see that you're taking an interest, and they'll be more inclined to talk in the future.

Topics with acronyms will be complex for people who don't know the subject. It's advisable to draw on your experiences to do what you do. If you're trying to convey something but using a lot of adjectives, the message will be lost, as the words don't relate to each other.

You must be honest and genuine when communicating with others - people have a sixth sense for telling when someone is being fake, which often makes them feel uncomfortable about talking to that person again. This can cause problems for your relationship if they misinterpret it (they'll think that you don't like them or that they didn't speak as much).

Another way to look at communication skills is that everyone makes mistakes, and we always learn. It's essential to learn from your mistakes and find new ways of communicating with others that work for you.

If you're having difficulty communicating with someone, try not to judge them harshly. Don't think badly of them or put yourself in the other person's shoes if they use inappropriate words or act aggressively toward you. Many people who have had difficult childhoods suffer from depression and low self-esteem - these are just some of the many mental health problems that can make it hard for a person to communicate effectively.

Perhaps the other person is under a lot of stress and feels like you do not understand them - this could be due to their way of communicating with others. If you don't know how to communicate with someone in your life, then take the time to educate yourself about what they're experiencing. This will help you learn how to communicate effectively with that person, so they feel better about sharing their thoughts and feelings.

To communicate effectively, we should first listen. By listening, we can give the other person our full attention and not let our thoughts cloud our judgment or interrupt what they say. They need to know that when they speak to you, you're taking an interest in what they have to say. To do this, repeat and summarize what the other person has said and see if this makes sense.

It's also important to compliment or express how we feel in the conversation so that the other person knows we're interested in them. If they're not being listened to and feel like nobody else is there for them, they won't discuss their feelings with others again.

You can also look at another person's face while talking - this will show that you're interested in what they have to say and will demonstrate your body language. Now practice these techniques, and you'll find that your conversations will become much more effective, and you'll be able to communicate with others in a way they'll understand.

Problems with communication are a common cause of arguments and conflict, but importantly they're also an opportunity for us to learn how to communicate better. When people don't like our ideas, new points of view, or what we have to say, it's essential not to show annoyance, anger, or irritation. Remember that most people won't get angry if you explain your position clearly and show them why it's the best course of action for them.

We can show someone we're interested in what they're saying by repeating what we've heard, paraphrasing, and summarizing their point of view. By looking at their face and body language when they're talking to us, we'll get a better idea of how they feel. If they're frowning or offering gestures, we should get in touch with them to see if something is wrong or ask why they are unhappy instead of ignoring it.

When someone says something difficult for us to hear or understand, then try not to react like this comes as a surprise because they may misinterpret our reaction if we do.

We should also be courteous when questioning a person's point of view, even if we disagree. This can help us see that they are serious about their position so we can take them seriously.

If someone is pushing to make an argument, we shouldn't fight with them but use our words to express the facts and let them know our reasons for disagreeing with them. When people are too hasty in making their point of view known, they may not have put enough thought into it. Before persuading them otherwise, we must understand why they feel strongly about the topic.

If someone is too aggressive towards us when we disagree with their ideas, we should try to deal with them rationally. By showing them that you're not willing to fight with them, you'll be able to get your message across without getting into a physical conflict. Understandably, they'll feel annoyed or hostile if they feel like they've been insulted, but this doesn't mean that you have to argue back at them or be dismissive of their feelings.

The goal of communication isn't just to express our ideas effectively and persuade the other person - it's also about working together as a team. We may not see eye to eye on every subject, but we can be united in believing that what we have to say is best for the greater good.

The essential part of communication is being transparent, honest, and genuine. If you appear to lack confidence at first, don't panic. It's better to start communicating effectively if this is not your forte than to hold back and leave someone confused about why you're being unresponsive.

Before communicating with someone else, prepare to demonstrate how much you care about them and your ideas. To be a more effective communicator, you'll need to think about what people are saying while listening to them. Pay attention to their intonation, tone, and facial expression - these will help you understand what the other person is saying.

If you listen well, you'll make it easier for the other person to talk to us and show us how they feel. We should put ourselves in the shoes of the other person we're communicating with to see how they're feeling.

When we listen carefully, we won't find it as hard to express our ideas or add something of value that nobody else can say - because when we listen well, we hear what they're going through.

What good reasons do you have NOT to communicate with someone?
Sometimes we can feel reluctant to talk to others, but this isn't necessarily bad. We should only speak to the people that want to hear what we have to say, and if we don't see this as necessary, then it doesn't matter if somebody else does.

For instance, we may feel that the people around us are not listening well enough. When they speak, they may not seem interested in what we have to say, or they may interrupt us during our conversations. If this is the case, we should keep our distance from them because they'll distract us from what we're trying to focus on.

There are other reasons why we shouldn't communicate with someone, like if we have no common interests with them or if it doesn't fit with the way that we want to live our lives. If we feel nervous when talking to someone because they're too aggressive, it might not be worth speaking with them whenever they want to talk to us.

Whatever the reason is not to communicate with someone, most of the time, it's better not to deal with them.

By looking at how other people communicate, you can learn how to do it yourself more effectively. If you want to influence someone positively, then it's essential to understand how you can get better at doing so.

By observing a person's behavior, you'll see what seems to interest them and what they're passionate about. You may also be able to see when they're having a difficult time in their life, but you can show that you care by asking them how they're doing or helping them in some way.

We can take lessons from other people as long as we're careful not to copy or imitate them - because this may land us in trouble. We should pay attention to the words and body language of someone else so we can use our own to communicate effectively with others.

Several resources are available to help us communicate well with others. Another way that we can gain insight into how to communicate well is by reading stories, studies, and books about famous writers and public speakers. By analyzing their behaviors and saying things the way they have, we can expand our vocabulary and become more expressive.

When we're ready to talk to someone else, our body language must be open so that the person isn't distracted from what we're trying to say. If we feel nervous, we should stand up straight and smile so that it won't make people uncomfortable.

We may not feel confident in how we speak about our ideas and influences, but that doesn't mean we can't change it for the better. It's easy to get distracted by other people or our thoughts, but if someone tries to explain something to us clearly, we should be open to listening.

If you're uncomfortable with how you speak, then you should talk to other people and try to engage them in conversation. By talking to others, we can learn how they express their ideas and respond when we talk back - so we must spend time talking with others so they can give us feedback on how effective our communication is.

When we're in conversation with someone else, we need to try and listen to what they have to say as much as they do. This can be challenging because we might feel they're not interested in what we have to say or are talking over us - especially if this is the case. By observing others, we can improve our relationships with others.

If our communication skills are unclear, then we shouldn't bother trying to talk about an issue because this may leave people confused. We should encourage these people so that they'll help us improve how we communicate our ideas and influences.

We can't change something we're not confident with, but we can be open to feedback from others to get encouragement. The best way to do this is by asking what people think about our ideas, but sometimes we should listen and ask if they have any advice or tips on how we should express ourselves.

If people around us don't want to talk, then it's probably better for us not to bother. It doesn't matter what these people say - all that matters is that they won't help us in any way and will distract us from what we need to focus on.

Here are some things we can do that can help us better understand and portray our thoughts and feelings during a conversation:

1. Formulate your thoughts. Come up with a list of areas you need to address and how exactly you will do so. Your friend or co-worker might feel the same, but they won't always know how they should be able to convey that to you, which is why it's your responsibility to ask them some questions.

2. Be aware of the situation. Are you in a position where your friend or co-worker might feel uncomfortable about what you're about to say? Are there other people around? Let them know that, no matter what, they shouldn't feel judged and that sometimes it's just easier if we can talk without others around us knowing our issues.

3. Don't get frustrated. If you find that your friend or co-worker isn't as forthcoming with their thoughts as you'd like them to be, try not to get frustrated at them. It's just not a great way to start a conversation.

4. Don't be afraid of confrontation. If someone is coming around and talking down to you or others, stand up for yourself and others! Please make your voice heard when necessary; it's better than pretending everything is okay when it isn't!

5. Take some responsibility for the other party's feelings. If a friend or family member complains about you to you, it's not their fault that they have problems communicating. Try to make them realize that communication is an essential skill, and try not to get too frustrated because they need some time to think of how they will handle things.

6. Be the bigger person. If someone gets upset and suddenly calls you names in an argument, don't take things too personally - it's tough when you receive hurtful remarks like this from a family member or friend that we're close with. Try saying something positive or polite to them after your argument has ended.

7. Listen carefully. If you are conversing with someone and ask them a question they've asked you to address but don't fully understand, then repeat it to them so that they know what you're trying to understand.

8. Make eye contact when speaking. It makes us feel confident and puts us in control of the conversation, which we think might usually make us blurt out our thoughts before we have time to process them properly.

9. Be specific. Don't make generalizations - if something is bothering your friend or family member, then tell them precisely what bothers you so that they can get directed towards the right place to find the source of their disagreement or upset with themselves.

10. Listen attentively. If someone is having a conversation with you and you have no clue how to respond again, listen intently for a couple of seconds before answering them. We feel it's best not to interrupt an individual when speaking to us, especially if what they say isn't much help.

Conveying your thoughts and feelings across different mediums is essential in our everyday lives as we seek to do well in everything we do. It enables us to give off the right impression and effectively express our emotions, opinions, and ideas, stay in touch with others and keep them updated with what's happening in our lives. The art of public speaking helps us to talk about our opinions in front of other people without getting tongue-tied. We rely on communication skills daily, and many problems can occur if we don't use them correctly. This can affect our personal and professional lives, and we often find ourselves unable to communicate effectively in certain situations.

Communication is an essential skill we all need to learn, whether agitated or lethargic, as it helps us feel comfortable in any situation. There are many types of communication skills training: you can know how to translate a written report into a formal letter; you can also take part in body language training, where you can gauge how other people react when you make specific movements. However, the most effective way of improving your communication skills is through the written word. Here are some things anyone can do to enhance their communication skills.

Formulate your thoughts. No matter the topic, you will find that you don't always understand what you hear. This is because there are two sides to every conversation; we must know what they mean when we listen to someone talking to us. By coming up with a list of points or issues you have with yourself or your life, then put these down on paper so that you can read them back later when you feel uncomfortable and need help. This cannot be easy at first, but it is the best way to ensure you take an optimistic life approach.

When you are having a conversation, make sure that you understand what the other party is saying to you before opening your mouth and answering. This way, you won't come across as ignorant or unintelligent and can feel comfortable speaking with those around you.

When it comes to what to say, try to be more tactful when communicating your feelings. If someone has upset you, don't pause for a second before telling them this, as this will allow them time to prepare a counterargument. It's always best to try and say something to make the other party feel better about themselves and then move forward.

When we learn new skills, it helps us to become even more confident than before. One thing that anyone can do to help improve their communication skills is to share them with others. The next time you're conversing with someone, have them write down what they think the other party is trying to get across. Then, ask them a question to clarify what they mean. This will allow you to practice your skills in front of others and help you feel more productive when communicating with others around you.

Chapter 13: How to Give Useful Feedback Without Offending People

When giving feedback to someone, you want to be constructive; yet your feedback can often come across as negative and even hurtful. It's easy to assume that people will react negatively, but it helps to remember that we all have different perceptions and reactions.

Here are some tips on how you can get the most sensitive feedback from the other person in your conversation:

1. Be specific

Use specific examples as much as possible; this will help them understand what they do that causes particular problems or makes certain outcomes happen. The more detailed and specific you can be, the less likely your feedback will be misunderstood. For example, instead of saying, "You are a sloppy worker," try, "You get distracted by listening to your radio when you work." If you don't know enough details about what or how the person does something, don't bother giving them feedback. It's not worth it.

2. Use I-messages

Avoid using you-messages when giving feedback. Instead of "You are a sloppy worker," try "I feel frustrated when I see your work piled up on your desk." Also, consider the other person's response if they received the same feedback. If they made excuses or became defensive, don't say it. You want to say things in a way that won't cause this reaction.

3. Make the feedback specific and non-judgmental

Focus on how something was done instead of why it was done (unless you know the reason is related to a personal value). For example, instead of saying, "Your work is sloppy," try, "I had trouble understanding your report. I think it can be more clearly written." The second statement focuses on how the work was done rather than why it was done. The less judgmental you are, the more likely people will listen to what you say.

4. Ask for clarification

If something isn't clear, ask for more details and examples before giving feedback. This shows that you're interested in understanding them (rather than just dumping on them).

5. State your observations and feelings about the incident in question

Be honest and discuss your thoughts on the incident if you give feedback. State what worked well and what could be improved. It helps to compare this to similar situations that have occurred in the past, but that isn't always possible. If it is difficult for you to talk openly about these things without being judgmental, don't feel wrong about verbalizing it in any way that makes sense.

6. Try not to react in anger

It's very tempting when someone does something that bothers or frustrates us to assume they did it with malicious intent wrongly. Try to be calm and ahead of the situation by asking yourself, "What is this person really thinking or feeling instead of assuming the worst?"

When someone's behavior or attitude bothers you, it can be easy to think about how it reflects on you. If you are standing in front of your boss complaining that the kitchen needs cleaning, some people might think he's talking about your work habits. You might think he's attacking you if you start to get angry.

When others are critical of behavior, they can often be required of your heart and mind. They may have difficulty accepting that the person they're talking to could also be doing their work poorly or taking criticism wrongly.

7. Don't be defensive

When you're defensive, it makes others feel uncomfortable and uneasy. When you're defensive, you focus on the problem, not finding solutions.

8. Give yourself a break

When someone is rude or cruel to you, take a break from it. Let the situation go, and don't dwell on how badly the person has hurt you. When you focus solely on what happened to upset you, your thoughts are likely to continue looping in that direction forever. Don't expect things to get better if they keep happening; instead, let go of thinking about them and move forward with your life to reach your goal or purpose.

9. Don't make excuses

When you're over-critical of behavior or negatively perceive someone, they can see that you're not concerned about their feelings or well-being. This makes it difficult to move on and be open-minded to the person's point of view.

10. Don't believe your own "facts" and assumptions about someone

When you think you know more than a person about what's going on in their lives, it can be tempting to jump to conclusions and make mistakes about how you think things are for them. This will result in an unnecessary gap between when what is happening and when your assumptions about the person take hold because of your defensiveness.

11. Avoid arguments

When you are defensive, and someone is trying to give you feedback, it can quickly escalate into a fight. When you argue about something, you focus on proving other people wrong. You look for flaws instead of finding solutions.

12. Remember that a compliment is no insult

When people feel unappreciated or taken for granted, they may not see the positive behavior as a compliment, condescension, or criticism. When you criticize someone, you're telling them what they are doing is wrong, harmful, or inadequate when it wasn't. When you understand how someone else sees your words, complimenting them instead can be perceived in a much more positive light.

How to avoid saying things that will make others feel judged or insulted

When someone behaves in a way that bothers or upsets us, we might try to motivate them by talking down to them and making them feel guilty. We might tell them how horrible they are, belittle them or make them feel guilty for something they didn't do.

While these types of comments are sometimes helpful and motivating, they can sometimes make other people feel judged. Also, when you talk down to someone this way, you usually project your feelings and thoughts onto the person. This is different from saying things like "I feel so frustrated because of what you did," rather than telling them exactly what's on your mind about the incident.

When you judge a person's behavior instead of using respectful language or expressing yourself with patience and kindness, you're trying to make them see themselves as inadequate or unworthy of love or respect.

There's nothing wrong with expressing yourself in an angry or upset manner. At times, being aggressive is a natural and necessary response to being hurt by someone. But, there are more productive ways to deal with adversity and situations you find unacceptable.

If you're having trouble being honest with someone in your life, the first thing to do is ask yourself what the benefits will be. When you firmly believe that they should know about their behavior now, you'll be better able to stick to your guns when it would be easier to give up on being upfront about how you feel.

When someone has hurt you or upset you, responding with aggression or anger isn't necessary because it doesn't make others feel hurt or guilty enough. You have to have compassion and say these things calmly and with kindness if they're going to get through.

Wanting what others have

When you feel angry, you may want to make a point of wanting something or someone else's possessions and things. You might want to try to intimidate or even hurt others by making them feel guilty for getting more than you.

Make sure that you recognize when something is your problem, not a person's

When you feel envious of what someone else has, it can be easy to think about how it reflects on you. If someone has something that you want, this might make you feel ashamed, inadequate, or worthless. You might think that all the problems in your life are because of how unworthy and irresponsible you are.

When something isn't going your way in life, it can be hard to accept that there are other explanations for the way things are then blaming yourself or other people. You might think things are only the way they are because of who you are and what you have.

When a person is sad, upset, or discouraged, it can be challenging to accept that what's going on in their life doesn't have to do with them but with how much they're struggling at the moment.

If you're going through a rough time and can't find any reason to feel bad, take a close look at yourself and all the ways you're contributing to getting what you want. Then, look at how you can change the situation to stop making yourself unhappy.

When someone feels unappreciated, lonely, or less-than, they may be working hard to make themselves feel better by creating a list of what's wrong with them and how they're not good enough. They might go through the same thoughts and feelings daily until they finally break down and cry. This reads like a conversation between them, and their self-esteem makes it seem like all the struggles in their lives are because of who they are.

When things aren't going well, it's helpful to write down your feelings about what's happening. It's also beneficial to recognize the other ways you can see your life going well. When you see the good things in your life, you won't feel like "all of this is about me, my flaws, and my problems."

Life is complicated enough without making it harder on yourself by focusing on others' potential shortcomings instead of what's happening in your own life.

Focusing on a bad situation or circumstance instead of seeing it through a positive lens can be hard to keep from feeling like a victim. This makes it easy for people to make jokes about how bad things are and how terrible the world is.

Most people who complain about what's happening in the world don't want to help change things for the better. Most people don't want to see things as unfair, unjust, or unnecessary. They want to point out how bad things are so they can feel better about themselves and so that people can feel bad for them instead of how dependent and helpless they are.

There's nothing wrong with finding joy in how a situation is going or how you're handling it. That doesn't mean that everything is entirely alright or that you shouldn't realize that there are problems in your life. It means that you can appreciate what you have and where you are instead of focusing on how bad your life is compared to others and how much you don't have.

Rather than focusing on your life's insufficient, think about the good things for you instead. Think about how your life could be if you were in control instead of blaming yourself or others for items that aren't going well.

When communicating, it is essential to do so calmly and with kindness. Instead of making yourself feel better or worse because of what someone else is doing or has done, notice how things aren't going well for you. Focus on what needs to change so that they do go well.

You'll likely feel angry or resentful when focused on what people are doing wrong. When you can separate yourself from other people and what they do, you can focus on what your life needs to look like to be positive.

Avoiding saying things that will make others feel judged or insulted is essential to keep in mind. If you think you might say something hurtful or offensive, it's better to say nothing. This can be easier said than done, but when it comes down to it, it's always better to be kind and open than harsh and judgmental.

If you're ever worried that your words will push people away or make them angry with you, then it's best not to say anything at all. People are often more willing to forgive someone who has apologized for saying something disrespectful than someone who has never said sorry.

When people feel uncomfortable around you, they may need to be defensive or put up walls, so they no longer have to feel threatened by you. If you think people aren't being open with you or have turned cold or hostile, you may want to be a little more careful when communicating with them.

When it comes to communicating, you don't need to avoid saying everything on your mind. Sometimes holding onto your thoughts and feelings can make it hard for others to get close to you. Sometimes ignoring what's on your mind is the first step to feeling more centered and peaceful.

If something isn't going well for you, try thinking about other ways that things could be going instead of focusing on how bad things are going for you now. It can help to think about the positive aspects of how you are handling your life right now instead of thinking about how it could be going better.

It can be challenging to want to feel different about your life when you're overwhelmed by all the things going wrong. However, focusing on how things could be better instead of how bad they already are will help you relax and get in touch with what you have.

When someone is feeling negative emotions, it can be hard for them to see a bright side or silver lining to what's going on. You won't see the same opportunities that people who aren't as emotionally invested see because your perspective differs.

When someone isn't in touch with their feelings or doesn't handle them well, they may use humor to avoid getting upset or taking something personally. You'll need to communicate your feelings without taking them too personally or putting them down.

When communication is good and open, it's easier for everyone to understand what's happening. When you're upset or upset about how someone else is communicating with you, it can be easy to go into defense mode and blame them for making you feel bad. However, things aren't always about someone else's intentions or desires.

When other people are trying to communicate with you, don't withhold your feelings, thoughts, or ideas so that you can feel better about yourself. When it comes to communication, it's essential to be honest and upfront so that others know where you're coming from.

As someone going through something difficult in life or who has lost someone they loved very much, it can be easy to feel like everything is hopeless and that things will never get better. Thinking about the good things in your life and how valuable they are instead of dwelling on the negative aspects of life and how futile they always will help lift some of the weight off your shoulders. It will also help you become more content and happy with the life that you do have.

Making it enjoyable to be around will help other people enjoy themselves more and make conversation easier. For some people, thinking about being kind and thoughtful can be difficult. However, when it comes to being patient with other people, it can be easier to ensure that you don't come across as rude or hurtful in your communication.

When someone is upset with you or disrespects your feelings, they may lash out at you or act like they don't care what you have to say or feel. However, if you interpret their behavior as them saying that they don't care, then you won't be able to get close to them.

When you think about what you want from a relationship or someone else and how it can help you feel more connected with them, it can be easier to stay open and have a good relationship. This will also help you keep in touch with your feelings and emotions so that you're in the right headspace to communicate effectively.

Try not to take other people's frustrations or struggles personally when they're frustrated with you or someone else. For some people, it helps them feel better and more peaceful when they get angry or sad rather than worse when they're upset.

When you're in a situation where you are trying to communicate some upbeat feelings to someone who appears hostile or angry, it can be easy to feel confused, uncertain, and frustrated. However, focusing on being calm and patient will help you get through the situation more quickly.

When someone is giving off vibes about how much of a perfectionist they are, it can be hard for them to make small talk with others because they don't want to seem like the wrong person. If people have too many expectations of themselves and feel like everything needs to be perfect always, it can make relationships harder for them.

Conclusion

Communication can be one of the most challenging skills for any individual. In today's highly connected society, those who have a solid foundation of communication skills can be better positioned for success. Be it through verbal or non-verbal language, communication skills are the building blocks for social interactions and professional relationships. There is significant value in effectively communicating with others and reading people like a book. Suppose you don't feel confident in your ability to read others or form meaningful relationships in your professional life. In that case, learning these skills is critical to developing as a leader and achieving career aspirations beyond just climbing the corporate ladder. While all people have unique values and skill sets, highly successful individuals have a few commonalities. If you seek to become a professional with high communication skills, the first step is to realize everyone you encounter has some vulnerability. Through this realization and by developing empathy for others, you can better connect with them on an emotional level. Ultimately, suppose you can establish rapport with someone by showing your interest in them as a person. In that case, you can more effectively communicate your ideas and get outcomes favorable to both parties involved.

It is common to hear people say they are bad at communication or don't know how to talk to people. These people often don't realize that one doesn't have to know something to be good at it. Some of the most brilliant minds in history have proven this to be true. These people demonstrated practical communication skills that are learned and can be improved with practice. Communication is about engaging others meaningfully and understanding the context of what is happening around you. No matter where you are and in front of you, you must develop positive relationships with those around you, your staff team, and department leaders to achieve career success.

Excellent communication skills require a correlation between what we say and what we mean through our body language. Some experts in communication even use gestures when they speak, trying to convey meaning with their hands as much as their voice. Taking the time to observe how others communicate can help you develop your body language and find your language style as well. It is important to note that communication is not always clear and straightforward. It can often be complex and challenging, especially when dealing with people from different cultures or backgrounds. However, building rapport and finding common ground through conversation will be more effortless as you become more aware of how others communicate. An excellent way to start a conversation with someone is by finding commonalities between the two people speaking rather than focusing on the differences that may exist between them. Depending on your goal for the interaction, there are various ways in which you can execute this task.

Since effective communication involves taking into account the context of what is happening around you, it can be used in any environment where practical leadership skills are required. Effective communication is so vital to leading a team that it has significantly improved performance. By developing strong communication skills and becoming more mindful of the context within which you speak, you can better promote the success of your team members and their lives.

While many believe there are no right or wrong ways to communicate, developing your unique style is always a good idea. Pay attention to what people say about you and consider how you want others to perceive your communication style. Consider what kinds of things come naturally to you when speaking with people. Then, choose to focus on those things. By becoming more aware of these issues, you can better communicate effectively and build long-lasting relationships with the people around you.

We have provided an overview of different types of communication and its other components. So that you have a basic understanding of the language used in the professional world so that when you are communicating with your colleagues and other people in any business place, both verbally and non-verbally, they will be able to understand what it is you want to convey.

We have provided an overview of different types of communication and its other components. So that you have a basic understanding of the language used in the professional world so that when you are communicating with your colleagues and other people in any business place, both verbally and non-verbally, they will be able to understand what it is you want to convey.

Communication is essential for any professional or individual. It is vital in building bridges and understanding others. When we communicate with another person, there is a background to ensure effective communication. It is not a one-way communication between two people. It is a two-way interaction. The goal of communication is to understand the other person. It begins with understanding your own emotions. A common trait of successful people is the ability to use their emotions as an asset that helps them better understand why they do what they do and potentially has a positive or negative outcome.

Communication can be further defined as expressing ourselves and our thoughts through words and gestures to get feedback from others, which helps us decide how to move forward in life (personal) or our work setting (professional). It is essential to realize that communication is not just how we express words but also involves understanding the type of communication used by others. This "communication" happens when we observe and understand non-verbal communication.

Here are some ways in which you can improve your communication skills:

Ensure you understand the message you're trying to convey before talking to someone. Be clear about what it is you want to get across to them. This way, the news will come across clearly in the conversation and help the other person understand better what you want from them.

Keep an open mind during a conversation with someone else, be open to new ideas and opinions, and be available for criticism. This way, if the message you are trying to convey to someone is not coming across clearly, then you will be more receptive and engaged in the conversation. Don't take it personally; use constructive criticism as a learning lesson.

Practice non-verbal communication whenever possible. Your non-verbal communication is essential to the message you're trying to convey when talking with others. Please pay attention to your body language, gestures, tone of voice, and facial expressions when communicating so that it comes across clearly what you want to get across in conversation.

Make eye contact when having a conversation with someone. It is a clear sign of interest in what the other person is saying and an excellent way to focus on the exchange. If you're unsure about the message you're trying to convey to another person, find out their views first, then explain yours. This uses active listening skills in your communication and taking notes from the other. This way, you can be more friendly and caring towards others.

Made in United States
North Haven, CT
03 August 2023

39902130R00075